Roger Bowen was born in Swansea and has lived and worked in London and East Devon for most of his life. He worked in industry in Exeter before retiring to Budleigh Salterton. During his career he was successively a member of the Engineering Industry Training Board, chairman of the Chamber of Commerce in Exeter, chairman of the EEF in the southwest, a governor of three schools, a member of the Employment Tribunals and for eight years he was the founder and organiser of the Budleigh Salterton Music Festival. He is engaged in charity work and has been a member of the local council. Since 1992 he has been chairman of the Devon Historic Buildings Trust during which time some 14 of Devon's iconic buildings have been restored to their former pristine condition.

Many interesting people have lived or are now living in Budleigh. Amongst these are Sir Walter Ralegh. the writers Fanny and Adolphus Trollope, the naturalist Dr Carter, broadcaster Alvar Lidell and, more recently, the broadcaster and journalist Sue Lawley and Booker prizewinning novelist Hilary Mantel, all of whom have contributed to Budleigh's colourful history. Now we meet in these pages the brilliant polymath Dr Thomas Nadauld Brushfield who lived in the town from 1882 until his death in 1910.

ROGER BOWEN

Lunacy to Croquet

The Life and Times of
Dr Thomas Nadauld Brushfield

First published 2013

www.rtbrbowen.org.uk

ISBN 9781 483935218

The story of Dr Thomas Nadauld Brushfield richly deserves to be told. He was one of those very rare people who truly deserve the epithet *polymath*.

As a pioneer in the treatment of lunacy he had few equals; as a bibliophile he was celebrated for his studies into the life and literary works of Sir Walter Ralegh.

Moving to Budleigh Salterton in 1882 he carved out a secondary career during which he offered 72,000 entries to the newly emerging Oxford English Dictionary and made many other contributions to archaeology whilst collecting 10,000 volumes for his personal library.

As an author he had interests as varied as medieval punishments and the church. When he died his loss was felt throughout Devon.

Contents

Preface

Many interesting and well-known people have lived in Budleigh Salterton. Few enough were actually born there. One famous exception is Sir Walter Ralegh whose portrait as a youngster was painted by Sir John Everett Millais as he sat with a fisherman on the beach wall. Note the spelling *Ralegh* because in deference to the subject of this biography it is accepted that Ralegh never spelled his name as *Raleigh*.

Most of the other celebrities who came to live here did so after a lifetime of work elsewhere. They came because the small town is unique amongst all others on the south coast of England in that it possesses a calming climate and rural charm that reminds visitors of the sunny days gone by when all the world was young. Many of them came to visit and stayed to the end of their days.

Such a one was Dr Thomas Nadauld Brushfield who chose Budleigh out of many other possibilities when he was forced to retire from a life spent in treating the insane in 1882. At last he could immerse himself in bibliography and in particular the life and works of Sir Walter Ralegh.

Dr Brushfield's interests were not confined to Raleghana, the term he invented to describe the work. Through his successful and inventive career from his early days in Whitechapel to the later periods spent in Chester and Woking, he wrote widely on subjects as diverse as medieval punishments, Roman remains, the history of churches, the Oxford English Dictionary and many more. His written output was prodigious.

Though he published widely and had many friends and collaborators he remains largely forgotten today. The reason for this cannot be that his works were parochial or trivial because this is evidently not the case.

The time has come for his praises to be sung and his work evaluated for others to enjoy.

Dr Brushfield possessed a delightful and interesting personality as all his many friends have testified. The systems he devised for the welfare of his patients have come to be adopted widely and he is still recognized as the foremost Ralegh scholar just as he was when he set down his pen for the final time in 1910.

If all the world and love were young,
And truth in every shepherd's tongue,
These pretty pleasuress might me move
To live with thee and be thy love.

The Nymph's rep;y to the Passionate
Shepherd - Sir Walter Ralegh

Chapter 1

1828

Beginnings

1828 was a wet and cold year. The winter[1] brought with it such low temperatures for so long that even the Thames froze. As Thomas and Susan walked the short distance to Christ Church in Spitalfields for the christening of their newly born son Thomas they must have been concerned that the inclement weather would be a further risk to their small family. This year they had already lost an infant son also named Thomas, born in 1827, to one of the ever present diseases in East London. These were days when large families were the norm and there was the expectation that women would bear a child every eighteen months. As they knew only too well, infant mortality, high everywhere was extremely high in London's East End.

Thomas and Susannah (Susan) came from Derbyshire and were married there[2], but had moved to London to help Thomas' trade prospects. Already, at the age of 31, he was beginning to carve out a successful career in the City as an oil and colour man[3].

The area of East London in which the Brushfields lived was described by Charles Dickens' biographer David Perdue[4]:

Imagine yourself in the London of the early 19th century. The homes of the upper and middle class exist in close proximity to areas of unbelievable poverty and filth. Rich and poor alike are thrown together in the crowded city streets. Street sweepers attempt to keep the streets clean of manure, the result of thousands of horse-drawn vehicles. The city's thousands of chimney pots are belching coal smoke, resulting in soot which seems to settle everywhere. In many parts of the city raw sewage flows in gutters that empty into the Thames. Street vendors hawking their wares add to the cacophony of street noises. Pick-pockets, prostitutes, drunks, beggars, and vagabonds of every description add to the colorful multitude.

Thomas and Susan lived in Church Street, depicted in 1676 as an unnamed road on the south side of the 'Spittlefield' running between Crispin Street and Red Lion Street. By the beginning of the 18th century it had acquired the name Little Paternoster and later Paternoster Row.

It was extended west to Bishopsgate in the latter half of the 18th century, the new extension cutting through Crispin Street, Gun Street, Steward Street and Duke Street (later Fort Street). This new section was called Union Street. It was renamed Brushfield Street on 25th February 1870 in honour of Thomas who by then had become a Justice of the Peace and a trustee of the London Dispensary in Fournier Street and a prominent Vestryman of Christ Church in Spitalfields, Stepney.

Thus, in the cold and wet November of 1828, Thomas Nadauld Brushfield was born into the world of stews and overcrowded streets that typified the London of the time.

In 1828 both Thomas and Susan had nearly 50 years left to them and they would spend all of them in and around the same streets even when they had become financially very successful.

In *Little Dorrit* Dickens describes a London rain storm:

> In the country, the rain would have developed a thousand fresh scents, and every drop would have had its bright association with some beautiful form of growth or life. In the city, it developed only foul stale smells, and was a sickly, lukewarm, dirt-stained, wretched addition to the gutters.

In 1831 the Brushfields had a second son, Richard, and this proved to be the full extent of their small family. They now had two boys to educate and by 1841 both of them were boarding with Mrs Stevens at her establishment in Buckhurst Hill, Chigwell in Essex[5].

Now very much a part of suburban London, in those days Chigwell was a rural village fairly close to the Brushfield home in Spitalfields, yet far enough away to avoid the miriad of diseases that brought death to so many of the poverty stricken families of East London. By now Thomas was becoming wealthy (when he died in 1895 he left a fortune of nearly £50,000).

As the century wore on, writers and artists began to produce increasingly sentimentalized images of children, emphasizing their angelic, adorable qualities. Yet despite such rhetoric, real reform did not come quickly. High infant mortality rates, inadequate schooling, and child labour persisted right to the end of the century, suggesting that many Victorians remained unconvinced that childhood should be marked off as a protected period of dependence and development.

How surprising then that Thomas and Susan Brushfield should Have adopted such a different view for their two boys.

Thomas and Susan were pillars of Christ Church so they were well aware that London churchyards were completely overwhelmed by the number of burials that were occurring. By necessity many would be on top of previous burials. Within a decade most central London churchyards had shut to any further burials and large civic cemeteries had opened in their place. The churchyards were viewed as places of disease and Londoners were pleased to see them turned into green spaces. [6]

The boys were destined for very different careers. Thomas was quicker to learn and was showing real intellectual prowess and a strong sense of independence, whereas Richard was ready to take on a trade, like his father. In later life Thomas soon moved away from the family home but Richard continued to live in Church Street for many years. Thomas would marry in 1856 near home in Stepney and Richard in 1865 also near home. Both lived to old age and both had families; Thomas with nine children and Richard with three from two wives.

The school both attended, run by Mrs Stevens in Chigwell, was large, with some fifty boarders registered in 1841. Facts are few for this period and it is not possible to observe how the boys' education was conducted between 1835 and 1845.

What we know is that Thomas was destined to become most successful at London University and at the London Hospital as a doctor recognized universally by friends and colleagues as brilliant and that showed in every aspect of his life.

He was a pioneer in medicine specializing in the treatment of lunacy, a bibliophile who wrote a multitude of papers, articles and books on a wide range of literary and archaeological subjects and a delightful fellow to befriend. When he died, in 1910, he left an estate valued at £16,100.

By contrast brother Richard left close to £30,000 when he died in 1904, which testifies to the profitability of father's oil and colour business.

The elder Brushfields came from Derbyshire; in Thomas' case from Ashford. Son, Dr Thomas, whilst living in Chester, investigated the name Brushfield and the small villages where he believed the name originated. Several of his papers on these subjects are listed in the bibliography.

As a final word on Thomas' and Richard's schooling, Mrs Stevens, headmistress, and Mr Stevens, proprietor, are listed in 1841 as schoolmistress and stockbroker in their large school house in Chigwell where they provided the education that gentile Londoners required for their older children. Thomas had not yet built sufficient wealth to contemplate the Rugby or Eton choice. Whatever the truth there seemed no brake applied to the progress of young Thomas in his chosen career in medicine. He achieved the university's matriculation in 1845 at a time when few enough were capable of achieving this standard.

Family history was important to Thomas Brushfield. Born[7] in the village of Ashford-in-the-Water, in Derbyshire, on the 16th of February, 1798, Thomas was the son of George Brushfield, of that village, and Anne, his second wife (his sole issue by his first wife being a daughter, Frances, married to Mr. Willliam Bramwell). His grandfather, descended from a family of very high antiquity in the county of Derby—the Brushfields of Brushfield— was Richard Brushfield, who, although but a village blacksmith, was a man of understanding, and had acquired some property by marriage.

The son, George Brushfield, was brought up by his maternal uncle, who, for some reason "cut him off with a shilling," and left his property to his brothers and sisters. Being a man of strong judgment and of more than average powers of mind, he rose above the disappointment, and became the "counsellor and friend " of his poorer neighbours, and the constant and respected companion of the village magnates.

He married, as his second wife, Anne (Aune), daughter of the Rev. Thomas Nadauld (successively incumbent of Great Longstone, Ashford-in-the-Water, Belper, Turnditch, and Kilbourne, in Derbyshire) and son of Peter Nadauld of Ashford, surgeon, and Margaret, his wife. George says she was

"fitted in every respect to fill a high and honourable
position in society ; she was a woman of strong mind, and was
possessed of extraordinary fortitude, perseverance, and sound
judgment. The reverses to which my father and she were
subjected (and they were very severe ones), she bore up against
and struggled through in a manner worthy the bravest and
greatest of her sex."

Her epitaph, literally a true one, says "Her life was a living lesson of piety, benevolence, and usefulness." She died on the 26th of November, 1855, in her 84th year, and her husband on the 25th of February, 1825.

They had nine children: Richard Nadauld Brushfield, baptized Nov. 9th, 1796, who died on the 13th of March, 1871, leaving among other bequests, the sum of £250, the interest of which was to be given annually to "such of the inhabitants of Ashford as the Trustees shall deem to be most needy and deserving" and irrespective of their religious opinions; Thomas Brushfield, and four other sons, and three daughters: viz., George Brushfield, who died in the United States; Joseph Blackden Brushfield, who died in 1849. and is buried at Ashford ; Benjamin Brushfield, resident in the United States; Peter Brushfield, who died in the United States ; Elizabeth Brushfield (married to Mr. Henry Gadsdon), who died in London ; Anne Brushfield, who died at the age of of nineteen, at Ashford ; and Margaret Brushfield, married to Mr. W. Darwent. [7]

Mr. George Brushfield lies interred in the graveyard attached to the now destroyed Baptist chapel, situated on the roadside from Ashford to Wardlow, not far from the Edge Stone Head. His son, Mr. Thomas Brushfield, placed there a gravestone to his memory, bearing the lines of his own composing; "the stone is now ruthlessly broken to pieces and scattered about."

Huguenot time line

31 October 1517   Martin Luther nailed his 95 theses on the door of the All Saint's church in Wittenberg, Germany

Autumn 1533   John Calvin experienced a religious conversion brought about by God and flees Paris

29 January 1536   Followers of new Protestantism were accused of heresy against the Catholic government

1536   John Calvin published his *Institutio Christianae Religionis* (The Institutes of the Christian Religion)

1545   The Massacre of Merindol - Francis I of France ordered the Waldensians of the city of Mérindol to be punished

28 January 1561   The *Edict of Orléans* is proclaimed to stop the prosecution of the Huguenots

17 January 1562   The *Edict of Saint-Germain* is promulgated and ensured limited tolerance of the Huguenots

19 March 1563   Peace of Amboise ends the First War of Religion

8 August 1570   Signing of the Peace of St Germain-en-Laye

23/4 August 1572   St Bartholomew's Day Massacre

6 July 1573   The Peace of La Rochelle and the *Edict of Boulogne*

13 April 1598   Signing of the *Edict of Nantes* where freedom of religion was given to the Huguenots and they also received equal rights to the Catholics

1629   The Merciful *Edict of Nimes* gave the Huguenots a certain right of existence but their political power was permanently removed

22 October 1685   Louis XIV revoked the *Edict of Nantes* and declared Protestantism illegal with the promulgation of the *Edict of Fontainebleau*

28 November 1787   The *Edict of Tolerance/ Edict of Versailles* is declared which partly restored the rights of the Huguenots

Chapter 2

1685

The Nadauld Heritage

Henri Nadauld, at the age of 32, left the town of his birth in the Santongue region of France, in L'ille d'Oleron, near La Rochelle and boarded a fishing vessel bound for England. He was a Calvinist protestant[1].

The year was 1685 and the Huguenots[2] were responding to the religious persecution that had been their lot since the revocation in October 1685 of Henry IV's Edict of Nantes of 1598, by his grandson Louis XIV, that made the practice of their faith almost impossible. The original intention of granting rights to the protestants in France, ostensibly to promote civil unity, was thus reversed and this drove an exodus of protestants to the protestant lands around France, many of them to England.

This was a difficult decision for Henri to make because his life in France was spent as a gentleman with few skills or qualifications to equip him for his new life. He had taken a keen interest as talented amateur in sculpture and this is the artistic trade he entered with considerable success.

He was born in 1653 to Simon Nadauld, had married Mary and already had three children. Making a new life in England would be difficult for him and his family. Though he was one of approximately

300,000 émigrés there was still the enormous challenge of language and customs. However, the evidence is that these new arrivals in England were made to feel welcome as persecuted protestants.

It made for a difficult year as Henri Nadauld settled in London where he had a yard and studio in Piccadilly and was active in providing garden and house sculptures and decorative features during the period 1690 until he died in 1723[3].

In 1690 he was responsible for sophisticated decorative carving and statues at two of the great English baroque houses. His son Pierre, born in 1685 in France, was naturalized in 1707 and is described in the records of the Huguenot church in West Street, London, as coming from 'I'lle de Oléron', near La Rochelle. He became a surgeon and raised a family in Ashford, Derbyshire.

Henri Nadauld worked at Hampton Court Palace in 1698, where he was paid £50 for plaster work in the Queen's closet in the water gallery. The shed provided for 'the 'Frenchman to burne his Plaister in' and the 'Squaring and laying two stones' for him 'to beat his plaster on' probably refer to Nadauld although the accounts spell his name 'Nadue'. Again he is almost certainly the 'Monsieur Noddo' who was rated on two houses in Portugal Street, Piccadilly, on 20 December 1697. His yard was near to such other statuaries as John Nost I, Edward Hurst and Richard Osgood. He was named 'Nedos' in the Castle Howard accounts.

By 1700 Nadauld had moved to Chatsworth where in July the carpenter was paid for making a shed for him and where he worked, inside and out, until 1706[4]. He produced ornamental details for the façades and garden sculpture under the supervision of Monsieur Huet, a Huguenot minister who acted as steward to the 1st Duke of Devonshire. Many of the other craftsmen were also Huguenot refugees. Nadauld worked also on the interior, providing a chimneypiece and figures for niches on the west staircase. One of his finest achievements at Chatsworth was a plaster relief of putti on horseback and acanthus foliage, on the coving of the west sub-vestibule. Such ornamental carving was usually supervised by the architect in charge, but six working drawings by Nadauld at Chatsworth indicate that he was responsible for developing his own designs. The design for the frieze on the west front, in black chalk on paper, shows pairs of tritons blowing conch shells and pairs of winged sea horses, their tails entwined or tied with ribbons to three-pronged tridents[5]. The drawing also relates to the great frieze on the south front at Castle Howard where Nadauld worked from 1704. His work at Chatsworth was sometimes mundane[5] but he also produced a wealth of mythological and allegorical sculpture.

An account of work done in 1703 includes three figures for the inner court in 'Roach Abbey stone', a building material considered by Wren to be second only to Portland stone. Nadauld's bill includes 'Charges to Roach Abbey' of 12/-, which suggests that he selected the stone himself. He was still working in the gardens in 1714, but largely on repairs to figures, cleaning statues before their repainting and on carving a pedestal and '2 Seafish heads for ye cascade', which sound as though they were replacements.

Meanwhile he retained his London yard and in 1704 won the commission to provide a mural monument to Lady Eland (grand-daughter of the Huguenot Marquis de la Tour de Gouvernet), in Westminster Abbey. Now dismantled, only the bas-relief survives, representing the deceased reclining on a plinth supported by cushions, with a mourning female figure in her left. It is signed 'Nadaud fecit'[6].

Nadauld was in Yorkshire working at Castle Howard from 1704-10, so that his work there overlapped with Chatsworth. Indeed one of his bills to the Earl of Carlisle specifies 'foure little figures called the foure Sezons made at Chattworths'.

Henri retired to Derbyshire, where he died at Ashford-in-the-Water, near Bakewell (on the Devonshire estate) in 1723. His name features in the Ashford Court Rolls where it is recorded that his death had occurred by the time of the October court but not before the June court of 1723.

Following the terminal decline of London's silk weaving industry at the end of the Georgian period[7], both Fournier Street and Brick Lane became established as the heart of the Jewish East End. Although there had been a small Jewish community in the East End for some time, a large number of Jews from Eastern Europe and Russia moved to Spitalfields in the 19th century and founded a thriving community. Many new schools, cultural activities and businesses were created, including the Jews Free School and the Jewish Chronicle newspaper (the oldest Jewish English language weekly in the world). In 1898 the Methodist Church at the eastern extremity of Fournier Street was converted into the Maz'ik Adath Synagogue.

This building had been constructed as a Huguenot Chapel ('La Neuve Eglise') in 1743-4, had also served as a Protestant church and would later be converted during the 1970s to become the London Jamme Masjid (Great Mosque) as the area then evolved to become the present day heart of the Bengali community.

This building's changing use in responding to the changing religious needs of the surrounding population over its 280 year long history is symbolic of Spitalfields' role in immigration and in providing 'refuge'. Upon a wall on the south side there is still to be seen the large sundial carved with the inscription "*Umbra sumus*" a quote taken from Horace's odes meaning "We are shadows".

Fournier Street also has the church of Christ Church Spitalfields at its western extremity, designed by Nicholas Hawksmoor, a former assistant of Christopher Wren, and built between 1714 and 1729. This Grade 1 listed building is widely considered to be the highest expression of English Baroque architecture[8].

The foundations were laid in 1714, and construction of the walls took place over the following years, although the upper stages of the tower and spire were not built until the late 1720s, and the church was finally consecrated on 5 July 1729.

Huguenot immigrants favoured this area of London and there are many references to the superb craftsmen who settled here. Though Henri Nadauld moved from London to Derbyshire to retire it is recorded that he kept his yard and two houses in Portugal Street, Piccadilly[9]. His family grew up in Ashford, Derbyshire very close to the small mining village of Brushfield.

Henri's son Peter (Pierre Nadauld) is recorded as living in the same Derbyshire village in 1724. His son, Thomas Nadauld, was born before 18 January 1727 and died 9 November 1807 at Ashford, at 80 years of age and his body was interred after 9 November 1807 at Holy Trinity Churchyard in Ashford.

He married Elizabeth Emery at Brewood in Staffordshire on 11 August 1763. Elizabeth was born before 1 April 1742 and died in November 1824 at approximately 82 years of age. Her body was interred 19 November 1824 at Ashford. Thomas was a priest in Great Longstone Derbyshire in 1755 and on 7 August 1764 he is recorded living at Brewood.

In the case of *Elizabeth Dorothy Nadauld Starbuck versus John Williams*, Thomas appeared as the deponent on 27 August 1792[10].

Thomas Brushfield and Elizabeth produced six children of which the third daughter, Ann Nadauld married George Brushfield.

George, who died in February 1825, was father to Thomas Brushfield, born in 1798, who became a very successful merchant in the city of London and who is recorded living in Church Street, Spitalfields in 1841. Thomas was, of course, father of the subject of this biography, Dr Thomas Nadauld Brushfield born in 1828 in Spitalfields.

Thomas, father, married Susannah Shepley who was born in around 1794 and who died in London on the 11 October 1865. Thomas and Susannah had 13 children of whom Thomas Nadauld Brushfield, was the second son.

The north side of the street was (and to some extent still is) dominated by the buildings of Spitalfields Market. It was renamed Brushfield Street on 25th February 1870 in honour of Thomas, by now a Justice of the Peace and trustee of the London Dispensary in Fournier Street. Much of Brushfield Street (except the 19th century buildings of Spitalfields Market) was altered in the 1920s - the London Fruit exchange was built on the south side in 1928 and further market buildings were constructed on the north side around the same time. These latter buildings were demolished in the 1990s and were replaced 2001-5 by the large office and retail development known as Bishop's Square.

Several 18th century buildings still survive on the south side of the street and most are now restaurants or cafes. The rear frontages of the Bishopsgate Institute (1895) are visible at the western end.

The career of Thomas Brushfield, merchant, is fascinating. He lived nearby at both 5 and 12 Church Street, Spitalfields, London, later renamed Fournier Street, where he is described in 1835 as "Thomas Brushfield, a prominent vestryman, after whom Brushfield Street was named" and who was also a trustee of no 27 Fournier Street , known as "The London Dispensary" until the NHS was formed in 1946.[11]

In addition to this he was a merchant of the city of London dealing in oils and colours. He died a wealthy man.

It is interesting to reflect upon the hugely important trade in oils and colours. Paint could be obtained from the ironmonger who usually also dealt in oils.

Thomas described himself as an "oilman" or 'oil and colour merchant'. Reginald Betts the chemist had the same wording in his advertisements and William Barker's stock list of his Market Hill premises for 1892 included prussian blue, spruce ochre, persian red, venetian red, indian red, purple brown, pale ultramarine, raw sienna, burnt sienna and red ochre as dry powders.

The paint was made from these basic pigments combined with a binder and solvent to ease its application. Linseed oil was the commonest binder and drying oil. This was ground with the pigment by hand using a muller (similar to a pestle with a wide base) on a stone slab. Turpentine was the main solvent and this would have been hard work when a substantial quantity was needed.

White lead was the most effective pigment for making white paint, and Barker had five hundredweight of it stocked in kegs. This was a period of change, as other kegs contained various colours that were 'ground in oil'.

Thomas Brushfield attended and supported his church Christ Church in Spitalfields very near to his home. Evidently much involved in church matters, he was chairman of the Christian Evidence Society, a religious society whose Reverend (Robert Taylor) was charged with blasphemy in 1827.

It is surprising that Thomas, a religious, successful and prosperous property-owning man, tolerated life in the filthy street conditions that were the norm during Queen Victoria's reign. The worst of these have now disappeared and much of the east end of London is today rebuilt or restored and occupied by upwardly mobile young people with good jobs and careers in the City. As they go about their daily lives maybe they reflect upon what conditions were normal during Charles Dickens' and Thomas Brushfield's time. This may have been a function of the problems of immigrant sections of the community such as the Jews, Russians and the Huguenots who had suffered the greatest indignities and discrimination in their own lands.

Just a road junction away from Church Street was the notorious Dorset Street. A vivid description of crime and vice in this street[12] is:

It was a street of whores. There is, I always feel a subtle difference between an whore and a prostitute. At least we used to think so. Prozzies were younger, and more attractive. Whores were debauched old bags. It teemed with nasty characters - desperate, wicked, lecherous, razor-slashing hoodlums. No Jews lived there. Only a few bold choots had the temerity even to walk through it. There were pubs every few yards. Bawdy houses every few feet. It was peopled by roaring drunken fighting-mad killers.

Booth's poverty maps of 1898 - 1899 show the area as in part black, indicating lowest class, vicious and semi-criminal.

Within a short distance of Church Street was the horrific scene of the "Jack the Ripper" murders of 1888, including five brutal murders[13]. All the women murdered were prostitutes, and all except for one - Elizabeth Stride - were horribly mutilated.

The first murder, of Mary Ann Nicholls, took place on 31 August. Annie Chapman was killed on 8 September. Elizabeth Stride and Catherine Eddoweson were murdered 30 September and Mary Jane Kelly on 9 November. These are often referred to as the 'canonical five' Ripper murders, although Martha Tabram, stabbed to death on 6 August 1888, is considered by some 'ripperologists' to be the first victim.

Violence to prostitutes was not uncommon and there were many instances of women being brutalized. Only a quarter of a mile from the scene of Catherine Eddowes' murder, the words 'The Juwes [sic] are not the men to be blamed for nothing,' were found scrawled on a wall in chalk, and it was suggested this was written by the killer. A police officer ordered the words to be removed, fearing an anti-Semitic backlash in an area with a large Jewish population.

Jack the Ripper was never caught and he is not thought to have killed again after November 1888.

Thomas Brushfield's family was a very happy one. His children distinguished themselves and one of them was particularly successful. Thomas, born in 1795, was hard-working, a characteristic he transferred to both his progeny. After a lifelong happy marriage with Susannah, when she died October 1865, Thomas had the inscription below placed on her grave. His was added in 1876:

HERE LIE THE REMAINS OF

SUSANNAH

FOR NEARLY FORTHY YEARS THE

FAITHFUL

AMIABLE AND BELOVED WIFE OF

THOMAS BRUSHFIELD

WHO DIED ON OCTOBER 11TH 1865

IN HER 71ST YEAR

IF VIRTUOUS DEEDS AND SPOTLESS

PURITY

WIN FOR A MORTAL SOUL A LIFE DIVINE

THEN MY DEAR SUSAN IT IS WELL WITH

THEE

A GLORIOUS DAY WHICH HAS NO NIGHT IS

THINE

ALSO

OF THE ABOVE NAMED

THOMAS BRUSHFIELD

The London Hospital

The Royal London Hospital was founded in September 1740 and was originally named The London Infirmary. The name changed to The London Hospital in 1748 and then to The Royal London Hospital on its 250th anniversary in 1990. The first patients were treated at a house in Featherstone Street, Moorfields in November 1740. In May 1741, the hospital moved to Prescot Street, and remained there until 1757 when it moved to its current location on the south side of Whitechapel Road, Whitechapel, in the London Borough of Tower Hamlets.[1]

Today the Royal London is part of Barts Health NHS Trust and provides district general hospital services for the City and Tower Hamlets and specialist tertiary care services for patients from across London and elsewhere. It is also the base for the HEMS helicopter ambulance service, operating out of a specially built roof area. There are 675 beds at The Royal London Hospital. The new building is the largest hospital in Europe.

Chapter 3

1831

School, University and the London Hospital

Though it made great sense for those who could afford the luxury to send their children into the care of safe houses set up for the purpose by entrepreneurs who combined bed and board as a means of making a gentile living. It is clear that the Brushfields were well able to afford the cost.

Many children in early Victorian England never went to school at all and more than half of them grew up unable even to read or write, although some did go to the Sunday schools run by churches. Children from rich families were luckier. Nannies looked after them, and they had toys and books. A governess might teach the children at home. Then, when the boys were old enough, they were sent away to public school. The daughters were kept at home and taught singing, piano playing and sewing. Slowly, things changed for poorer children too. By the end of the Victorian age all children under 12 had to go to school. Now everybody could learn how to read and write, and how to count properly.[1]

In the Stevens establishment in 18411 there were some 50 boys of whom Richard and Thomas aged 11 and 13 respectively were listed by name. The school was housed at Woodford House, Buckhurst Hill where the head of the house was Barbara Stevens who described herself as "wife of Francis Stevens, schoolmaster".

In 1851 the Stevens family had moved to Strawberry Lodge, Carshalton, Surrey where they housed a medley of young children and servants. All the children are listed as having been born at Chigwell or Loughton which is a village close by. Francis W. Stevens is not now a schoolmaster, but a stockbroker. In the same census one of the school's assistants , George LeMoine, is in the workhouse and listed as "former schoolmaster". So much for the need for professional qualifications to teach; then anyone could set up a school.

The Stevens establishment was the school of choice for those who could afford it. The one attended by Thomas and Richard was short lived and there is no further mention of it after the 1841 entry.

Charles Dickens in 1840 wrote about a similar house:

Those who like to read of brilliant rooms and gorgeous furniture would derive but little pleasure from a minute description of my simple dwelling. It is dear to me for the same reason that they would hold it in slight regard. Its worm-eaten doors, and low ceilings crossed by clumsy beams; its walls of wainscot, dark stairs, and gaping closets; its small chambers, communicating with each other by winding passages or narrow steps; its many nooks, scarce larger than its corner-cupboards; its very dust and dulness, are all dear to me. The moth and spider are my constant tenants; for in my house the one basks in his long sleep, and the other plies his busy loom secure and undisturbed. I have a pleasure in thinking on a summer's day how many butterflies have sprung for the first time into light and sunshine from some dark corner of these old walls.

Thomas, now 17, was successful at shool and in his studies and progressed well because he was able to qualify for the University of London (initially established to act as an examining body for its colleges and other 'approved institutions) in 1845. The University had awarded its first degrees in 1839 to 29 students.

Thomas matriculated with honours at the university in 1848. He then studied medicine at the London Hospital. Created in September 1740. The London, as it became known, came into being when seven men met in the Feathers Tavern in Cheapside to found what was originally named The London Infirmary[2]. Like other charities, the London Infirmary was founded by professional men, businessmen and philanthropists but the London Hospital 'was intended for the sick poor among the merchant seaman and manufacturing classes': the East End community of the time.

The hospital's surgeons and physicians trained pupils, by taking them into the hospital, discussing with them the patients' illnesses and sometimes allowing them to administer treatment. This method of teaching was combined with lecturers and anatomy classes, taken outside the infirmary until 1785, when the London Hospital Medical College (the first hospital-based medical school in England), was founded by William Blizzard and James Maddocks.

The custom of the operation bell was still in use in Thomas' day: the bell, together with the bell of 1757 that hangs in the hospital entrance, was made in the Whitechapel Bell Foundry. Before the introduction of anaesthetics in 1846, it is reputed to have summoned attendants, mostly medical students, to hold surgical patients still for the procedures.

In the 18th Century death from starvation was common[3]. Many women died in childbirth and still more children died in infancy. Plague had disappeared from London with the Great Fire and the black rats which spread the disease, but there were regular outbreaks of smallpox, dysentery, typhoid and typhus (or gaol fever). Medical treatment was limited to quinine for ague (malaria), mercury for syphilis and laudanum (opium and alcohol) for pain relief, while ineffective methods like bleeding, purges, vomit induction, artificial sweating, cold bathing and restriction of food and water were promoted by most physicians.

Surgery, whilst based on improving knowledge of human anatomy, was limited by terrible difficulties in the 18th and early 19th centuries4. Anaesthetics were not used to relieve pain in surgery until the 1840s, so operations had to be very rapid. The first operation conducted under anaesthetics (chloroform) at The London Hospital was in February 1847. Artery forceps were not introduced to stop bleeding until 1870 and surgeons relied on tourniquets (tight bands), cauteries (hot irons) and ligatures (silk threads) to prevent blood loss.

The surgeon's greatest problem was his ignorance of germs and infection. Wounds became infected and surgical instruments introduced germs. Many patients survived an operation but died later of blood poisoning. In the 1870s surgeons began to appreciate the importance of hygiene and preventing germs in surgery by using antiseptics like carbolic acid.

Thomas John Barnardo, became a medical student at the London in 1866 and set the up the first of his Dr Barnardo's homes in Stepney Causeway.

Thomas Brushfield entered 'The London' in 1845, and won three gold medals – for chemistry in 1847, awarded by the governors of the hospital; another for chemistry in the session of 1846 - 1847; the third for physiology in 1849, beside other honours. He became M.R.C.S in 1850 and graduated M.D at St. Andrews University in 1862.

Thomas was appointed as house surgeon at the London Hospital which was the highest grade he could have obtained following training.

In 1851 Mr Thomas Nadauld Brushfield, left 'The London' to join Dr Millar at Bethnal House Asylum, London as house surgeon.[4]

A friend and colleague, Dr J H Moreton, wrote of him:

He entered the London Hospital in October, 1845, which at that period was only a small school and a small hospital, but it was convenient for his purpose as he could live at home. He was, I need not say, industrious, for that remained with him all his life and he was successful in so far, that he carried away several gold medals for class work , and at the end of his terms became M.R.C.S. and L.S.A., the usual qualifications of those days. Finally he was appointed house surgeon, as being the highest honour the authorities of the hospital could confer.

In 1851 Brushfield was living in lodgings attached to the London with a small number of other doctors and hospital workers. Father, Thomas, with mother, Susan, were in Church Road, Spitalfields, living with brother, Richard, now in business as an oilman with his father. There were two servants, Emily and her daughter Sarah aged 39 and 21 living in the house.

The years 1843 through to 1851 were exceptional for the literature produced: Charles Dickens published A Christmas Carol; Jane Eyre and Wuthering Heights came from Charlotte and Emily Bronte in Yorkshire; Marx published his Communist Manifesto and Tennyson was appointed Poet Laureate. As his later literary achievements demonstrate, Dr Brushfield was undoubtedly fundamentally influenced by the writers of the time.

Inspection of records of criminal prosecutions at the Old Bailey show that the London[5] was the first port of call for medical expert witness and there are numerous examples to be found of young house surgeons appearing to give evidence. Young Brushfield appears in some of these cases. One of them involved a nearby lodging house keeper who was attacked and stabbed by one of his clients who interfered with his desire to make a rapid exit.[6]

After working at the London, Thomas got experience at first hand of the conditions prevalent in the famous or infamous Bethlem Hospital for the insane. The hospital was then situated quite close to home in the building that now houses the Imperial War Museum.

The conditions then were frightful. For a penny a visitor could inspect the wards. They were even allowed to bring with them a stick with which to poke and tease the unfortunate patients then chained in cells or to their filthy beds!

For Lord Shaftesbury6, advancement in the proper provision of asylums and more humane treatment for lunatics ran alongside other reforms concerning child labour in factories, factory reform, women labourers, and improvements to the working conditions of chimney sweeps and barrow boys. Therefore progress in the care of the mentally ill was part of a wider context of a growing agenda for charitable, benevolent reform, which had started to inform social policy within the governing classes of Britain in the mid-nineteenth century. Lord Shaftesbury led the campaign for lunacy reform, and then subsequently headed the Lunacy Commission, from its foundation in 1845 until his death in 1885. By the mid 1840s, Shaftesbury already had detailed experience of reforming lunacy law (Bethlem Enquiry) and it was a cause he championed consistently throughout his long and varied career. Towards the end of his life Shaftesbury regarded the work he did for the Lunacy Commission as one of his greatest achievements. Shaftesbury's pride further emphasises the charitable principles which underpinned much social reform during Victoria's reign.[7]

The Parliamentary Acts of 1845 marked significant progress in mental health legislation, as it fundamentally changed the treatment of mentally ill people from that of prisoners to patients. The shift from 'private misfortune' to 'public concern and action' was significant. The Acts effectively forced every local authority to set up a County Asylum; they were duty bound to provide care for their mentally ill paupers. In the mid- nineteenth century, when the Lunacy Act and the County Asylums Act were first introduced, it was hailed as one of the great moves toward compassionate social reform and as a 'triumph of public benevolence'.

The view of the Victorian asylum is now almost a wholly negative one, but at the time of the establishment of County Asylums, these institutions were seen as being at the very forefront of modern medical treatment and founded on nineteenth century progressive ideals of psychiatry. The new hospitals were designed specifically for the care of the insane, in which both legislators and the medical profession supported with more humane views on dealing with patients.

Both the Lunacy Act of 1845 and the County Asylums Act stipulated that an asylum should be placed in a spacious countryside location, but comparatively close to an urban setting. The notion behind this was to provide the patients with access to a secure village community in which to successfully convalesce.

At Fulbourn Hospital (first established as the County Pauper Lunatic Asylum for Cambridgeshire, the Isle of Ely and the Borough of Cambridge) the location was chosen carefully with this specification in mind. Fulbourn was built between the Cambridgeshire villages of Fulbourn and Cherry Hinton, south-east of the centre of Cambridge. Fulbourn Hospital had the ideal rural setting, with close links to two villages yet near enough to the more populated city of Cambridge. Again this proviso underlines the compassionate ideals attached to the legislation. It was one of the theories advocated in Victorian psychiatry that a pleasant environment was vital in aiding the well being of the lunatic.

Providing access to fresh air in a rural area was viewed as beneficial and a means of a cure for a wide range of ailments.

Whatever our negative views are of the Victorian asylum today, the attempt in the 1840s to improve the care of the mentally ill were a stark contrast to the treatment they had previously endured. Victorian theories on mental health were far more benevolent than their predecessors. The mentally ill were mainly treated harshly and often barbarously. The prevailing belief was that madness was a result of moral weakness, leading to a moral insanity and such a diagnosis was commonplace.

A combination of ignorance, fear and superstition left little or no refuge for the sick. Vulnerable people were left to roam the towns and countryside starving, perishing and neglected, some were left to languish in workhouses or cast indefinitely into jail. Individuals were often permanently chained in manacles, naked and kept in appalling conditions. During the eighteenth century it was a leisurely pastime in London to go to Bethlem Royal Hospital (Bedlam) to ogle the lunatics. For a mere penny, visitors could look into their cells, view the mad and be entertained by their antics. [7]

By the nineteenth century there was still a long way to go in terms of modern psychiatric care and abuses often still occurred. However, the main ethos behind the Acts of 1845 and the establishment of the County Asylums was to try and curtail the atrocious treatment that the mentally ill previously endured.

A kinder approach to mental health was backed up by new ideas in psychiatry, as well as a growing interest in public philanthropy, and charitable concern for the less fortunate. For example, when Fulbourn Hospital opened its doors in 1858, it specified the regime would be liberal and it regarded itself as an institution that followed a staunchly idealistic treatment programme of 'non-restraint'. Even kindness itself could be a cure for a mind afflicted by madness. Pauper lunatics were no longer unlawful criminals languishing forgotten in prisons but seen as patients who were unwell and who now belonged to the domain of medicine, psychiatry and palliative care; this was the beginning of the medicalization of mental health.

The task of the Lunacy Commission was to establish and carry out the provisions of the act. The Home Secretary oversaw the Commission and the task it set was, among other things, to inspect and evaluate the plans for establishing new asylums on his behalf. Hospitals had to be registered with the Lunacy Commission, there were to be printed rules and regulations and each institution had to have a resident medical attendant.

Also under the act, patients lost their right of access to the courts to challenge their detention. According to the new Act only the commissioners could review detention or the County Visitors sanctioned by the commission.

The County Visitors were officials who were vested with the power to act in place of courts as the organising authority that monitored asylums in the name of the commission. By enshrining within Government law bureaucratic processes, which awarded power to the commission, the patient on entering the asylum lost their right to access the courts and protest about their incarceration. Patients were firmly, to use modern parlance, 'in the system'.

The Commission also had the task of collecting, collating and analysing information on the treatment of the mentally ill in the newly established hospitals. By creating a network of new County Asylums the notion was to give the commission the power to keep tabs on and monitor the conditions and practices at the asylums as well as introducing a systemised body able to scrutinize and regulate the treatment being given to the patients. The Commission also worked upon relocating some patients from prisons, County Gaols and workhouses so that they could be treated in the newly established asylums. It was a huge task, which set in motion a wealth of paperwork and a plethora of bureaucratic processes.

The nineteenth century approach to psychiatry, that had once seemed so progressive and which had fed the reform of the Lunacy Laws gradually came to be viewed as increasingly outdated and inappropriate. The Victorian idealism underpinning their foundation had long since slipped and indiscriminate abuses of the sick was once again rife.

Once again, County Asylums were increasingly viewed as virtual prisons. The County Asylum became a place that inspired fear and horror in many people's minds, which further perpetuated the stigma attached to mental health. There were more advances in the field of psychiatry; alongside additional Government reform and the suitability of the old County Asylum system was eventually questioned.

Its demise began in the early 1990s when the old mental hospitals were gradually closed in favour of the current model of an integrated community care system which liaises with specialised NHS mental health units.

From the first liberal acts initiated and developed between 1808-1812, along with the dual acts of 1845 and later the Lunacy Act of 1890, the County Asylums formed the backbone of in-patient mental healthcare. It was only when Care in the Community was introduced that the asylums were forced to close or became re-appropriated as smaller specialised mental health units.

However, when the 1845 Acts made it obligatory for every county and borough in the United Kingdom to provide or erect a purpose built Asylum to house the mentally ill, it was part of a huge leap forward in the care and provision of such patients. The establishment of the County Asylums should be seen as part of a wider agenda of liberal social reform, where charitable concern and public debate translated into real legislative change, which in turn provided a major step forward in the treatment of mental health. In comparison with the past, a more humane view of mental health was held by the Government, who in wider context of reforming social policy had the power and clout to initiate changes in the law, which attempted to improve the lives of the sick and the destitute.

The experiences of Bedlam did not deter the young Dr Brushfield though. It is easy to see that the backgournd described above was inspirational as well as modernising. For the next 30 years, until forced to retire, he pursued a career in asylums bringing to each place new and sympathetic forms systems of treatment that forbade the use of restraints.

The decade was also notable for its other events: Fox Talbot produced his first photographs; the penny post started; Euston Station opened and Queen Victoria ascended the throne and married.

All these happenings influenced Dr Brushfield. He became interested in photography as his published work shows and he travelled the country by means that were not dreamed of in his grandfather's day.

Christ Church, Spitalfields

This Anglican church was built
between 1714 and 1729 to a design
by Nicholas Hawksmoor. Situated
on Commercial Street, in the
London Borough of Tower Hamlets,
on the eastern border and facing the
City of London, it was one of the
first (and arguably one of the finest)
of the so-called "Commissioners'
Churches" built for the Commission
for Building Fifty New Churches,
which had been established by an
Act of Parliament in 1711

Chapter 4

1827

Christ Church, Spitalfields

In 1827 in London one of those interesting events happened that cast the spotlight upon the beliefs held by churchmen and the seriousness with which they treated those who transgressed. Thomas Brushfield, upcoming merchant of the city, oil and colourman and vestryman of Christ Church, Spitalfields was much involved in one of these.

The *Trial of the Reverend Robert Taylor upon a charge of blasphemy, with his defence as delivered by himself, before the Lord Chief Justice and a special jury, on Wednesday, October 24, 1827*

was the indictment.

The Brushfield family in Derbyshire were committed Christians, not least because of their Nadauld Huguenot ancestry. One of the family living in the village of Brushfield, Thomas Nadauld, became a priest in 1755[1]. In that small comunity Ann Nadauld would have known the Brushfields well and she married one of them, George Brushfield, in Ashford in around 1795. Thus the Nadauld protestant connection was established.

Against this background, when Thomas and Susan Brushfield moved to their new home in Church Street, in 1824 in London's East end, they quickly became involved with the church. The parish church. Christ Church, played a very important part in their lives and that of their sons. As befitted a very successful merchant, being a supporter of the church was to exercise the same funtion today of doing good works and being involved in charitable activity.

Why was the case of Robert Taylor so important and why was Thomas so intimately involved?

Robert Taylor[2], who lived from 18 August 1784 - 1844 was widely known in the 19th century as "the Devil's Chaplain". He was born in England and became a member of the College of Surgeons in 1807. Undergoing a religious conversion, he was ordained an Anglican priest in 1813 and became curate at Midhurst. But he lost his faith about five years later when a parishioner exposed him to rationalist writings. Resigning with a splash, he took out an advertisement seeking employment, which spelled out his loss of religion. Bowing to his mother's pleadings, he briefly returned to the ministry, but was expelled for giving deistic[2] sermons.

In 1826 Taylor opened a deistic chapel. He flouted church authority by wearing his episcopal garments when giving his deistic lectures. That year he was sentenced to a year in jail for one of his sermons.

In 1827 he was arrested for blasphemy, and during the year spent in Oakham jail he wrote two books: *Syntagma of the Evidences of the Christian Religion* (1828) and *The Diegesis: Being A Discovery of the Origin, Evidence, and Early History of Christianity, Never Yet*

Before or Elsewhere So Fully and Faithfully Set Forth (1829).

He and oft-jailed freethought publisher Richard Carlile paired up and distributed a handbill inviting Cambridge students to hear

"The Rev. Robert Taylor . . . and Mr. Richard Carlile . . . present their compliments as Infidel missionaries, to . . . most respectfully and earnestly invite discussion on the merits of the Christian religion."

This made a deep impression on student Charles Darwin, who, in later delaying the release of his theory of evolution, took into account their treatment at the hands of Cambridge authorities.

Taylor and Carlile were thrown out of town and authorities even revoked the license of the landlord who had rented to them. He wrote a pamphlet called *"The Devil's Pulpit"* (1831), an energetic denunciation of New Testament dogma in which Taylor complained of "this tax-burthened and priest-ridden country." In 1831, he was again convicted of blasphemy, was sentenced to two years in prison and was fined £200.

Samples of his writing in *'The Devil's Pulpit"*:

. . . [the profession of the Christian faith is] a system of the grossest hypocrisy, a fashionable villainy, a licensed swindle, cheat, and trick. . . .

. . . go to church and chapel, you fools, - listen to the parson, and shut your eyes, and open your mouths, and see what God will send you.

Never was the day, never, in all the tide of time, in which
such mighty efforts were made to keep mankind in ignorance;
never were any clergy on earth, Pagan or Papistical, so
opposed to the diffusion of knowledge, so desperately afraid of
it, and so bitterly hostile to it, as the Protestant clergy, both of
the established church, and the dissenters of the present day, in
this metropolis.

In 1833, he edited a London publication, *Philalethian*. When
Carlile published Taylor's weekly lectures as *The Devil's Pulpit*,
Taylor again was charged with blasphemy and was sentences to two
years in Horsemonger Lane jail.

In jail, he was badly treated but, upon being released, married a
wealthy woman. He then moved to France, became a surgeon, and
never again published another word about unbelief. Thomas
Brushfield as chairman of one of the meetings at which Rober Taylor
spoke was there and gave evidence.

A shortened published account of the trial follows:

This being the day appointed for the trial of the Rev.
Robert Taylor, at an early hour a large concourse of persons,
amongst whom there was a considerable portion of well-
dressed and youthful females, were seen assembled ontside the
doors of the Court. Shortly after nine o'clock every seat in the
Court was occupied, and the benches of the Counsel even were
largely intruded on by the miscellaneous multitude. The

reverend defendant, accompanied by a large escort of friends, then entered the Court, and took his place on the attorney's seat, immediately in front of that of the King's Counsel. His appearance attracted all eyes : he was arrayed in the flowing gown of a clergyman ; his neat clerical hat was conspicuously borne in his hand, an eye-glass depended from his neck, and the little finger of either hand was ornamented with a sumptuous ring, his hair was arranged in the most fashionable style; and a pair of light kid gloves completed the elegant decoration of hls person.

Amongst those whom curiosity had attracted to the Court were Baron Graham, who occupied a seat on the bench, and Lord Sefton, who obtained accommodati-on amongst the King's Counsel.

At half-past nine o'clock Lord Tenterden came into Court. The Special Jurymen were then called ; six only answered to their names.

The Attorney-General, who was leading Counsel for the prosecution opened the proceedings and the Jury was completed by common Jurymen.[3]

There is no room in these pages in which to present the evidence heard by Lord Tenterden though the events recorded above, show how involved were prominent business men of the City in matters of faith and religion.

Thomas Brushfield, in 1827 was a member of the Christian Evidence Society that met every Thursday in various halls in the City of London. The objects of the Society were to debate and inform anyone who cared to attend, about religious subjects. On the date in question the society had invited that colourful character, Robert Taylor, once a priest, to debate, in public, his views about the New Testament. He presented his arguments:

1. The scriptures of the New Testament were not written by the persons whose names they bear
2. That they did not appear at the times to which they refer
3. That the persons of whom they treat, never existed
4. That the events which they relate never happened

Robert Taylor was described as the Orator of the Areopagus and Chaplain of the Society of Universal Beneficence.

Apparently the audience included several young persons even including some young girls. The effect upon those that heard Robert Taylor was dramatic.

Thomas Brushfield was a prominent member of the Christian Evidence Society who, said Beadle Collins, rang a bell to start the meeting. He was attired in a black gown and introduced Robert Taylor. Collins and Brushfield observed that as each proposition was introduced there was raucous outcry and laughter.

Both Collins and Brushfield gave evidence about the content of Taylor's oration and a vigorous examination and cross-examination followed.

The outcome was that Robert Taylor was found guilty by the jury of six and committed to prison.

There were many other interests that marked Thomas Brushfield out as a man of property, responsibility and even wealth.

Christ Church[2], Spitalfields was built between the years 1714 and 1729 as part of the church building programme initiated by the Fifty New Churches act of 1711, backed by Queen Anne, which was implemented by four different Commissions.

At the time, there were fears that 'godless thousands' outside the City of London had no adequate church provision, and that non-conformists – including large numbers of French Huguenot silk weavers – were moving into Spitalfields and bringing their non-conformist worshipping ways with them.

The Commission appointed to build the 50 new churches stipulated that the new buildings should have tall spires so that they would tower above the smaller, non-conformist chapels! The idea was to fund the work through taxes on coal coming into London, although monies ran low in about 1719 and building progressed fitfully.

One of the two surveyors employed by the first Commission, at an initial rate of £200 per year, was Nicholas Hawksmoor – a Nottinghamshire-born architect[4] who had worked with Sir Christopher Wren since his late teens. Of the 12 churches completed (out of the projected 50), six were the work of Hawksmoor, and Christ Church was his masterpiece.

An important Brushfield contribution was the founding of the London Dispensary[5]. The building was constructed in 1858 to house the Eastern Dispensary. This had been started by a group of doctors in 1782 and with the Duke of Wellington as its president, it was one of the first attempts to provide medical treatment to the poor of the area.

The dispensary relied on voluntary contributions from charitably minded people and the inscription *voluntary contributions* still remains on the building today.

The dispensary closed in 1940 owing to wartime difficulties and was converted into a public house in 1998.

Brushfield was also active in supporting the poor and destitute of the area. He was a trustee of the workhouse and the orphanage. A description of the conditions that pertained is provided by a visit of a physician[6] to inspect the premises[6]:

In going over the Whitechapel workhouse I was struck with the statement of the fact, that, out of 104 children (girls) resident in thy house, 89 have recently been attacked with fever. On examining the dormitory in which these children sleep, my wonder ceased. In a room 88 feet long, 16½ feet wide, and 7 feet high, with a sloping roof rising to 10 feet, all these 104 children, together with four women who have the charge of them, sleep. The beds are close to each other ; in the beds there are never less than four children, in many, five ; ventilation of the room is most imperfect. Under such circumstances the breaking out of fever is inevitable....

I was likewise struck with the pale and unhealthy appearance of a number of children in the Whitechapel workhouse, in a room called the Infant Nursery. These children appear to be from two to three years of age ; they are 23 in number ; they all sleep in one room, and they seldom or never go out of this room, either for air or exercise. Several attempts have been made to send these infants into the country, but a majority of the Board of Guardians has hitherto succeeded in resisting the proposition.

In the Whitechapel workhouse there are two fever-wards; in the lower ward the beds are much too close ; two fever patients are placed in each bed ; the ventilation is most imperfect ; and the room is so close as to be dangerous to all who enter it, as well as most injurious to the sick. In the upper fever-ward the beds are also much too close, but here the beds are single, and the ventilation is better. The privies in this workhouse are in a filthy state, and the place altogether is very imperfectly drained : there is not a single bath in the house.

Who was to blame for this? Certainly not Thomas Brushfield. His efforts were directed at improving conditions wheresoever he could. What is surprising is that people of wealth and achievement in life lived cheek by jowl with the unfortunate, the diseased, the destitute that lived in the parish of Christ Church.

Chester County Lunatic Asylum

The Cheshire County Lunatic Asylum opened in September 1829, under the auspices of the 1808 County Asylum Act which allowed for Justices of the Peace to levy a county rate in order to establish asylums to accommodate pauper lunatics.

Initially the Asylum had accommodation for 90 patients, men in the south wing and women in the north. The patients slept on straw bedding and used unbreakable bowls, horn feeding mugs and wooden spoons. To look after these patients there were 12 attendants and a matron but no regular night nurse and the two doctors (L I Jones & Mr W Rose) were neither resident nor full time.

Chapter 5

1852

Chester County Lunatic Asylum

Thomas Nadauld Brushfield was appointed house surgeon to Chester County Lunatic Asylum in 1852 and was the first resident medical superintendent from 1854. He remained in Chester until 1865.

A colleague in Chester writes:

Mr T N Brushfield, as he then was, came to Chester Asylum as house surgeon - the medical superintendent of the day being Dr. Llewelyn Jones, who was non-resident.

In 1854, the superintendent resigned and was appointed consulting physician, while his house surgeon became resident superintendent, and began with keeness the splendid work of his life.

He suggested to the committee of magistrates that before taking up the duties of his appointment he should have a holiday: this he used in taking a tour through the northern counties, and minutely inspecting every asylum within his reach, carefully noting even their smallest detail of furniture, fittings, bedding, carpets, crockery. mugs, jugs, spoons, knives, forks, etc., etc.: mixing with all official from the highest to the lowest. acquiring a knowledge of rules and regulations; watching the treatment of patients by those in authority, and by those working under them

Laundry work, kitchen work, garden and farm, all came under his own personal observation for future guidance. Cheshire County Lunatic Asylum was opened in 1829 on a site in Liverpool Road.

The original building, which housed 90 patients, was designed by William Cole, junior, county architect, and was erected under the direction of the county magistrates.

The staff who dealt with the pauper lunatics was headed by the medical superintendent who had own house and servants, the principle aspects of his job being concerned with the administration and legal aspects of the running of the asylum. There was very little medical treatment available for mental illness except for sedatives such as bromide & paraldehyde so the assistant medical officers were principally dealing with the general health of the patients. Due to this lack of medical treatment the attendants were appointed principally for their practical skills such as farm work, carpentry, laundry and cooking, because the asylum was, as far as practicable, a self sufficient organization. Attendants were poorly paid and lived in with part of their pay consisting of free lodgings, food and laundry.

The average number of patients during 1860 was 300; rising to 600 in 1890 and again to 900 by the year 1900.[1]

On taking up the duties of his appointment, he, without any hesitation or delay, began to do away with every form of mechanical restraint; the straight waistcoat was at once abolished, and instead of it, when restraint was required, it was always done efficiently by the attendants and warders. This new treatment, of course, required some patience and teaching, but it was soon understood by the staff that no violence was to be used, and no unnecessary pain inflicted, and certainly no injury was to result. The only mechanical restraint, and by which even the most violent patient could come to no harm, was the padded room, and that, in time, was very rarely required.

To Victorian physicians and reformers, the eighteenth century lunatic asylum was a fearful place. In What Asylums Were, Are, and Ought To Be (1837), the psychological physician W.A.F. Browne indicted the condition of those:

'left to linger out a lifetime of misery, without any rational attempt at treatment, without employment, without a glimpse of happiness, or a hope of liberation'.

The lunatic, he continued, was:

'terrified or starved into submission, lashed, laughed at, despised, forgotten.'

The great objects of such 'wretched and comfortless prison-house[s]', Browne concluded, were to confine and conceal the insane rather than to treat and cure them. This was especially the case in private, often unregulated institutions. Under the guidance of canny physicians and entrepreneurs who recognised the potentially lucrative rewards to be had by a properly-managed private asylum industry, the private madhouse business - the 'trade in lunacy' - flourished. The most attractive of these enterprises, the ones that were designed to reassure and to appeal to the fee-paying middle and upper classes, were given comfortable names such as the 'Retreat,' the 'Home,' or the 'Lodge.'

'The relatives and guardians of private asylum patients believed that these institutions offered a far better, more personalized environment in which to treat their lunatic relatives. Discretion was paramount. Private asylum proprietors did not publicize their case books, print details of cures or release the names and details of patients to prying inquisitors. While the apparent 'privacy' of private licensed establishments reassured some, the private nature of these sites of care led in time to accusations of financial corruption, administrative irregularities, and illegal, abusive treatment practices. As stories of the abusive treatment of patients reached the public, and when interested observers and reformers began to question the entire system of private care, it was not only the profit behind the private asylum which was heavily criticized, but also the perceived threat to the civil liberties of patients that such institutions embodied.'

In this climate of mistrust, the belief gained ground that the sane were being sequestered in private asylums as though they were mad.

In the eyes of many people in Victorian England, this was a horrifying scenario in which the asylum proprietor and the patient's family and friends colluded wrongfully to confine an individual.

It was not long before the idea of wrongful confinement became linked, in the popular imagination, with the whole private madhouse business. Claims of wrongful confinement as early as 1763 led to the first public investigations into mad-houses and the emerging trade in lunacy. Despite the public's concern, it took over a decade for the Parliamentary Select Committee's investigation to turned into the 1774 Act for Regulating Madhouses. Limited in its outlook, and only covering madhouses within a seven-mile radius from the capital, this act gave the state no power to revoke licenses, and made no provision for pauper lunatics. Its only significance, which was of no benefit to the insane themselves, lay in alerting the public to the existence of illegal detention of sane persons in madhouses.

Dr Moreton:

For something like fourteen years at Chester, Dr Brushfield so established himself as an authority in the treatment of the insane[2], that his opinion in respect of this disease was deservedly recognized by all who were conversant with the subject of lunacy. In order to fully carry out his ideas, a most complete system of entertainments, concerts, soirees, plays and dances was established. Though no recreation room was at first available, one was very soon fitted up-I think the dining room - and although at first the space was limited, so great was the necessity, and so keen the wish on the part of the members of the staff, nurses and attendants to help, there was no fear of failure.

In a short time a new chapel was built in the grounds, the old chapel was transformed into a recreational room, and all went on splendidly. With a good room, a good attendance soon followed, friends from Chester volunteered to help in every way, and other friends came to mix with those of the patients who were able to join, and with the attendants, so that the entertainment at the Chester Asylum were sources of enjoyment not to be forgotten.

The[1] effect of the mental conditions of many of the patients was most marked; those capable of improvement, appreciated and looked forward to these Tuesday evenings with great and increasing delight; some, in the interval, having incurred the displeasure of the superintendent, lost their evenings enjoyments, and could only regain it by better behavior. In a soiree of mixed entertainments a few even of the patients were allowed to play, or rather to think they played, some musical instrument; the violin was rather a favourite, or the flute, the concertina also in the hands of one of the patients "quite brought down the house," and the performer was so excited, that it was difficult to bring the piece to an end. Dr. Brushfield himself, besides being an organiser of these festivities, was more than than an ordinary good conjurer, as many still living will remember, not only the ordinary tricks, with the cards, disappearing coins, inexhaustible bottle, and hat, etc., but even fish in vases full of water, and living people disappearing out of boxes to nowhere. In addition to all this, the Doctor was an actor of very considerable power, a singer of very wide range, a writer of special research and correctness, and a very good friend.

No one could fail to see that the system of treatment, in the hands of Dr. Brushfield was bound to gain ground; it is now the foundation of treatment in every English system. During Dr. Brushfield's residence at the asylum he took the greatest interest in several pieces of antiquarian and archaeological research in Bridge Street and Watergate, Chester. In 1868, he published a delightful little book on the Roman remains of Chester, the illustrations of which are from the author's own pen, and are characteristic of his genius in this direction.[2]

Before leaving Chester in 1866, Dr. Brushfield had taken his degree of MD at St. Andrew's University; he had also taken several degrees in husbandry.

To put this in perspective, in the 18th and early 19th centuries, people with mental illness could be cast out from society. If harmless, they were ignored and left to cope as best they could; if considered dangerous, they were confined, sometimes in degrading conditions. Confinement was a way of removing them from society; treatment was rudimentary and mechanical restraint was sometimes necessary. The mental illness of King George III helped to focus public and political attention on the problems of the mentally ill – politicians and doctors began to be more active and asylums were built. This led to the foundation in 1841 of the Association of Medical Officers of Asylums and Hospitals for the Insane.

On the 5th August in 1857 Mr Thomas Nadauld Brushfield (who had not yet taken the degree of MD) married Hannah Davis in Spitalfields. Both bride and groom were born and bred in East

London and Thomas Brushfield JP and his wife of 20 years still lived in Church Street as did their second son, Richard, now a partner in his father's oil and colour business.

Both the younger Thomas and Hannah were 29 years old and they were ready to start a family. Their first child, confusingly also named Thomas was born in 1858 followed by Percy Richard in 1861 and Florence in 1862. The young family was now growing up in Great Boughton, Cheshire.

Times were changing. in 1859 Darwin published his Origen of Species, the first trams were evident on the Streets around Spitalfields and the American Civil War began. Mrs Beeton published her invaluable advice to homemakers in 1861. London Underground opened in 1863 and Alice in Wonderland was published. The first woman doctor qualified in England.

Susan, beloved wife of Thomas and mother to Dr Thomas and brother Richard died, in Spitalfields, in 1865 on the 11 October of that year.

Dr Thomas Nadauld Brushfield left Chester for a new appointment near Woking in Brookwood, Surrey in 1866.

As Dr Moreton writes in 1911:

> With household goods and with several trusted attendants, Turner and the two brothers Williams, who continued with him for the whole period of his stay at Woking he took his leave of Chester, both to the regret of every official connected with the asylum, and also a host of friends in the old city, who had, during his residence among theme, been attracted by his

wonderful personality , his genial comradeship , and his desire to enter into all the means of usefulness to Chester as well as to his patients.[3]

Chester Archaeology Society

The Society's name has varied over the years, alternating between the concise and the comprehensive. The first was the 'Chester Architectural, Archaeological and Historic Society'. In 1886 this was altered to 'The Archaeological and Historic Society for the County and City of Chester and North Wales'. After a number of minor changes over the years in 1966 this was finally reduced to the simple 'Chester Archaeological Society'. Despite these alterations, the geographical scope and range of interests of the Society have remained largely unaltered.

Together with the Chester Society of Natural Science, Literature and Art, the Society founded the Grosvenor Museum, opened in 1886, and played a key role in establishing Chester's renowned collection of Roman inscriptions and sculptures and in safeguarding the archives of the county. It has sponsored many archaeological investigations and was largely responsible for ensuring the preservation and display of Chester's Roman amphitheatre and for preventing the demolition of numerous of historic buildings

Chapter 6

1867

Wider Horizons

In 1868, as he left Chester, Thomas Brushfield completed his little book entitled The Roman Remains in Chester which was published in 1871. His other publications that date from his time in Chester are listed in the notes. Most of these were published by the Chester Archaeological Society.

Throughout his time in Chester Thomas was developing a range of interests in literature and literary pursuits. He became the president of the Chester Archaeological Society in 1863 and stayed in touch with the Society over the years often visiting for annual meetings and other functions.

From the list of his works the immense range of his interest will be obvious. Apart from the demands of his work with patients he embraced archaeological research in Roman Chester on the Rows and Bridge Street, odd details of old Cheshire punishments, and a particularly interesting and simple-to-understand survey of Roman remains in Chester. All the listed publications may still be viewed at the Chester library and the book is still available from antiquarian booksellers.

His manuscripts and drafts for some of these works are still to be consulted in the Devon Records Office and make intriguing reading. His small and delicate handwriting is easily readable, in contradiction of the popular belief that the script of doctors is usually scarcely legible. In three bound volumes Brushfield lays out a detailed catalogue of the terrible punishments dealt out to the unfortunates of the day and in previous decades[1].

He meticulously extracts printed descriptions and sketches and provides many of his own to illustrate, for example, the red-hot pincers used to tear at the flesh of convicted criminals and such other punishments as the cutting out of tongues for the crime of gossiping too loudly, the ducking stool for women who made the mistake of speaking out loudly; all inflicted with relish by law.

Is there an unhealthy interest here? If so it is mitigated by his daily inspection of the horrible treatments commonly given to lunatics in asylums that still existed through the land. These volumes of punishments were written in Chester but published much later in Exeter. The work must have occupied many hours of detailed inspection of manuscripts and records that he was able to access through his professional work.

It is now that Thomas Brushfield adopted his system of working with complicated documents and literary works that he was discovering and preserving for later study. In more than 40 commonplace books - covering 40 years[2] - he meticulously recorded a work schedule in columns in minute detail on each page. He then crossed through each task when completed so as to leave the original description still legible. Most of the commonplace books still survive and are available for inspection today; they strongly resemble spreadsheets in layout.

As if these activities were not enough, Brushfield also developed a keen interest in photography that flowed from the work of Fox Talbot, who published his first pictures in 1840.

As Brushfield says of the work of Sandor L Gilman entitled *Seeing the Insane: A Cultural History of Madness and Art in the Western World*. He writes:

> I have not had the opportunity of reading or knowing the contents of Dr. Diamond's paper on photography as applied to the treatment etc of lunacy beyond the ordinary newspaper article; but I have found notwithstanding my imperfect attempts, that the patients are very much gratified at seeing their own portraits and more particularly when associated with a number of others on a large sheet of Bristol board and hung up as an ordinary picture in the ward.

After his first appointment in Chester Dr Brushfield continued to develop these and many other interests.

A huge new opportunity now opened as Surrey magistrates publicised their intention to build a new asylum, near Woking, at Brookwood. Much influenced by his growing reputation for the innovative work he was doing in Chester, Dr Brushfield was now approached to become superintendent and offered a free hand in the detailed design of the buildings and in every aspect of equipment and layout of facilities.

Though he had been very happy in Chester the chance of putting into practice his new ideas was too good to miss. He moved to Brookwood in 1865.

Meanwhile Dr Brushfield joined Thomas Bateman in his excavations in Derbyshire. In *Vestiges of an Antiquarian -Thomas Bateman and his Network*:

> Thomas Bateman inherited a taste for antiquarian studies from his father, William Bateman. A small percentage of objects in the Bateman Collection were originally part of William Bateman's collection, and many of these had their origins in local 18th- to early 19th-century antiquarians such as Rev. Samuel Pegge, White Watson and Major Hayman Rooke. Notes and published material by these Derbyshire antiquarians as well as his own first excavations of 1843 were collected by Thomas Bateman in a manuscript, Collectania Antiqua (Bateman 1847) found in the Sheffield Museums archive.

These reports were eventually sumarised in Bateman's first book, *Vestiges of the Antiquities of Derbyshire* (Bateman 1848) along with his own early excavation diaries. It is quite clear from Thomas Bateman's early work that his excavation methodology was influenced by well-known archaeological pioneers in Britain, particularly Richard Colt Hoare.

Lunacy to Croquet

Broadwood Lunatic Asylum, Woking

Brookwood Hospital at Woking in Surrey, was established in 1867 by Surrey Quarter Sessions as the second County Asylum, the first being Springfield Asylum in Tooting. A third asylum followed in 1882 at Cane Hill in Coulsdon in the eastern part of the county.

Designed by architect Charles Henry Howell, the principal asylum architect in England and architect to the Lunacy Commissioners and Surrey County Surveyor from 1860–1893,[2] the 'Brookwood Asylum', as it was originally known, was renamed 'Brookwood Hospital' in 1919.

From its opening on 17 June, 1867 until its closure in 1994, Brookwood Hospital was the leading mental hospital for the western half of Surrey, occupying a large site at Knaphill, near Brookwood. The hospital had a dairy farm, a cobbler's workshop, a large ballroom, and had its own fire brigade, gasworks and sewage farm. It employed the services of many local businesses.

Chapter 7

1864

Brookwood Asylum, Woking

Dr Brushfield's distinguished medical career was devoted to the study and treatment of mental diseases, in which department he was eminently successful. After being Medical Superintendent of the Chester County Asylum fourteen years, he was appointed Medical Superintendent at Brookwood Asylum in 1865.

Dr Fleming said of Thomas Brushfield:

> Full of zeal in his work and with a remarkable capacity for organization and management, Dr. Brushfield's talents found ample scope in the necessary extension of accommodation for the insane. He was a first-rate asylum superintendent, and practically introduced a new era in the treatment of the insane. His kind and thoughtful solicitude for the welfare of his unfortunate patients caused him to promote schemes for their entertainment which have been adopted in every asylum since that time[1].

Opened as a second Surrey County Asylum in June 1867 Brookwood received 328 patients 1867. On an 1873 map it is on Knaphill Common, south west of "Woking Convict Prison".

"The site was selected for cheap land and the Surrey Justices purchased 150 acres in 1860 for £70 per acre. The asylum was designed to be self sufficient with its own gas works, sewage plant, a water tower with reservoirs holding one million gallons of water, the four acre Home Farm, and recreational areas. Occupational therapy was born and able patients put to work on making items the asylum needed such as furniture, baskets, rugs, tools, etc. and growing their own food. It was all commendably enlightened for its time and with building extensions the number of inmates grew steadily from 670 in 1875 to 1500 in the 1930s. Besides providing a great deal of local employment for nursing and maintenance staff the hospital became a major social centre for the district, organising fetes,shows, weekly dances, sports events and fund raisers."

Edward Sackett[1] (born 1840) was admitted to the workhouse infirmary, Russell Street, Bermondsey on 14 November 1874, but moved to Brookwood Lunatic Asylum a week later. In the 1881 Census, Edward is listed as Henry Sackett.

There were several assistant medical officers: James M. Moody (27 unmarried) and James E. Barton (36 unmarried) who was being visited by George H. Barton (aged 28), a stockbroker, and Thomas "Waklay" (medical student aged 29) who is probably Thomas Wakley (1851-1886), grandson of Thomas Wakley founder of the Lancet, who became joint editor with his father in 1886.

Edward Sackett was one of thirty patients moved to the Berkshire asylum in 1882 to relieve overcrowding at Brookwood.

His condition was described as "unimproved". Brookwood's contract with Berkshire expired in 1884, when Edward was moved to the new asylum at Cane Hill.

Dr Moreton observed:

It was fortunate that the committee of magistrates when they appointed Thomas had not yet completed the building, for then it was possible for every provision being made for carrying out fully all means necessary for a non-restraint system. The recreation hall was built under his own direction and has an ample stage complete with wing, slides and machinery: a splendid floor, mirrors, pictures, and vases, seats and indeed everything that could be required for concerts, plays, dances and entertainments of all sorts. The ideas that gave rise to these festivities in Chester were the same though here with fuller development: friends and neighbours came again and again, county people jostled with residents, friends and strangers helped especially in the winter months to carry out the ideas of recreation. A very special determination was also kept in view to carry out all the arrangements without any of the expenses falling on the rates of the county - entertainments were from the first self-supporting, and the only cost was for the building itself.

Brushfield was a most successful medical superintendent who brought great changes to Brookwood as a result of his experience in Chester and his earlier revulsion at the conditions that pertained in Bedlam.[2]

It is not necessary to say that could be done for the institution was done. Brushfield was happy in his work in every direction.; he had the confidence of the magistrates, a staff in whom he could place trust and confidence, something like 2,000 patients, and 200 attendants and servants and there were also the garden and the farm with the necessary men working them. So, for something like 16 years he, as an autocrat in his own domain, knowing well his own mind, carried out in full his own ideas of the treatment of the insane without restraint. There were no bars to the windows, in every room there were mirrors, pictures and vases within easy reach of anyone, pianofortes and billiard tables in several rooms, and to go through the place at any time, the most perfect order.

Above all Brushfield believed in the essential goodness within his fellow man and if they are mentally afflicted then they must be treated with compassion and offered not only medical help but also a means of living life at the institution in which they were unfortunate enough to be incarcerated. There the similarity to a prison must end. It is necessary to occupy the mind of the patient with uplifting and challenging activity.

Dr Moreton continues:

Thomas Brushfield was convinced that this must mean a meticulously planned environment. When he knew that he would be appointed to the Brookwood asylum he insisted upon the final construction being conducted according to his views and this was done. As a result the Brookwood Hospital was produced accordingly and this is where he was able to conduct experiments in the treatment of the mentally afflicted patients that proved very effective.

He was interested in many aspects of the environment he wished to produce. Later on the Cottage Hospital was erected in the grounds on a plan devised entirely by himself. Whilst at Chester he had abolished the use of straps, collars, strait waistcoats and other apparatus of a like nature and had them all burnt in the asylum yard by his orders. He also introduced amusements for the patients, brightened the wards with pictures and inaugurated dances, concerts and theatricals for thier benefit: as he himself excelled in these accomplishments, he often took part in the performances.

Brushfield comments on his hobby of photography:

In our worst female ward I have had a (photographic) positive (on glass) framed and hung up for nearly eighteen months, and it has never been touched by any of the patients, although nearly all know whom it represents. Last week a patient, who was formerly on of our most violent cases, begged for a portrait of herself, that she might send it to her son, who was in Ireland, to show how much better she was.

In the case of criminal lunatics, it is frequently of great importance that a portrait should be obtained, as many of them being originally of criminal disposition and education, if they do escape from the asylum are doubly dangerous to the community at large, and they may frequently be traced by sending their photograph to the police authorities (into whose hands they are most likely to commit): the photographs would cause them to be identified, and secure their safe return to the asylum.

The use of the photograph for recording the appearance of the insane raised questions about the access of the photographer to patients. While artists were permitted to sketch in the asylum during the eighteenth and nineteenth centuries, with the reform of the asylum the patient was no longer seen as the legitimate object of the curiosity seekers; rather, new emphasis was placed on the patient's privacy.

There were other ways of attracting the interest of the patient community. Dr Brushfield had long been interested in the stage and had produced and acted in a number of plays and presentations throughout his training in London. Now he promoted plays and entertainments and these became popular, not only in the asylum, but also in the wider community around Brookwood. [2]

Dr Moreton :

Not much survived from these (stage) productions but Thomas Brushfield carried this theme on for the rest of his life. Whilst in Chester Brushfield had a great interest in two other non-medical spheres: he conducted archaeological digs in or near the ancestral home of the Nadaulds in Ashford-in-the-Water and the village of Brushfield, both locations with mining and mineral extraction roots. It is no coincidence that they are both in Derbyshire very close to the place of work of Henri Nadauld in the eighteenth century at Chatsworth.

But Thomas' greatest interest, and one which he carried to the end of his days was in bibliography. What spare time he had was devoted to an enormous range of literature both of the region in which he found himself and more widely.

His time in Brookfield came to a very unfortunate end. He was respected and indeed much loved for his vibrant efforts on behalf of his patients and the surrounding community. How sad was it that he was involved in a violent incident not of his making.

Dr Moreton knew and spoke with a witness to the event:

One day he was conducting an inspection of the wards - something he did on every day to satisfy himself that all was well with the patients and their treatments and medical needs. As he entered the word containing the most violent patients he did not see one of them hiding behind the ward door with a bottle in his hands. Without warning he was struck down by a blow to the head of such severity that he fell immediately unconscious to the floor. There was little that anyone could do to prevent this and so he was carried way to his house nearby to recover.

This he did not do. He lay for weeks in a coma and there were fears for his life. Eventually, after many months of recuperation Dr. Brushfield decided that he could not expect to continue in his career at Brushwood in the way in which he would have wanted. The governors tried their best to persuade him differently but to no avail. A man of principle, as always, he decided that he was not able to perform his job in the way he wanted.

So ended Dr Brushfield's most successful career that spanned 40 years of which 16 years were spent at Brookwood. he was voted a generous pension of £700pa and left Surrey for Devonshire where he spent the remainder of his life.

Many tributes of high esteem came from the Surrey magistrates and all with whom he had been connected. He was a member of the British' Medical Association and of the Medico-Psychological Association. He was also a member of the British Archaeological Association, a Fellow and Local Secretary of the Society of Antiquaries, and a well-known Freemason, having held the rank of P.P.G.S.W. of Surrey.

In a sense, though, the unfortunate happenings in 1882 that ended his medical career provided a sound basis for this brilliant man's further career in bibliography and as an author.

Lunacy to Croquet

The OED

More than 600,000 words, over a thousand years

The Appeals are a new part of the Oxford English Dictionary website where OED editors ask for your help in uncovering the history of particular words and phrases. They ask if evidence for the use of words is available to assist with words and phrases.

In this way the modern work is similar to the *crowdsourcing* favoured by Sir James Murray and anwered by contributors such as Dr Brushfield.

Chapter 8

1864

Bibliography and the Oxford English Dictionary

Thomas Brushfield was intimately associated[1] with one of the most exciting and influential literary projects when members of the Philological Society of London decided, in 1857, that existing English language dictionaries were incomplete and deficient, and called for a complete re-examination of the language from Anglo-Saxon times onward, they knew they were embarking on an ambitious project. However, even they didn't realize the full extent of the work they initiated, or how long it would take to achieve the final result.

The project proceeded slowly after the Society's first grand statement of purpose. Eventually, in 1879, the Society made an agreement with the Oxford University Press and James A. H. Murray to begin work on a New English Dictionary (as the Oxford English Dictionary was then known). It was this development that provided the engine for Dr Brushfield's interest in the dictionary.

There is a most interesting coincidence because it transpires that Dr Brushfield was not the only lunacy specialist involved in contributions to the dictionary.

The Surgeon of Crowthorne: A Tale of Murder, Madness and the

Love of Words is a book by Simon Winchester that was first published in England in 1998. It was retitled *The Professor and the Madman: A Tale of Murder, Insanity, and the Making of the Oxford English Dictionary* in the United States and Canada.

It tells the story of the making of the dictionary (OED) and one of its most prolific early contributors, Dr. W. C. Minor, a retired United States Army surgeon. Minor was, at the time, imprisoned in the Broadmoor Criminal Lunatic Asylum, near the village of Crowthorne in Berkshire, England. The 'professor' of the American title is the chief editor of the OED during most of the project, Sir James Murray.

Murray was a talented linguist and had other scholarly interests, and he had taught in schools and worked in banking. Faced with enormous task of producing a comprehensive dictionary, with a quotation illustrating the uses of each meaning of each word, and with evidence for the earliest use of each, Murray had turned to an early form of *crowdsourcing* - enlisting the help of dozens of amateur philologists as volunteer researchers.

The new dictionary was planned as a four-volume, 6,400-page work that would include all English language vocabulary from the Early Middle English period (1150 AD) onward, plus some earlier words if they had continued to be used into Middle English.

It was estimated that the project would be finished in approximately ten years. Five years down the road, when Murray and his colleagues had only reached as far as the word 'ant', they realized it was time to reconsider their schedule. It was not surprising that the project was taking longer than anticipated. Not only are the complexities of the English language formidable, but it also never stops evolving. Murray and his Dictionary colleagues had to keep track of new words and new meanings of existing words at the same time that they were trying to examine the previous seven centuries of the language's development.

Murray and his team did manage to publish the first part (or 'fascicle', to use the technical term) in 1884, but it was clear by this point that a much more comprehensive work was required than had been imagined by the Philological Society almost thirty years earlier.

Over the next four decades work on the Dictionary continued and new editors joined the project. Murray now had a large team directed by himself, Henry Bradley, W.A. Craigie, and C.T. Onions. These men worked steadily, producing fascicle after fascicle until finally, in April, 1928, the last volume was published. Instead of 6,400 pages in four volumes, the Dictionary published under the imposing name *A New English Dictionary on Historical Principles* – contained over 400,000 words and phrases in ten volumes. Sadly, Murray did not live to see the completion of his great work; he died in 1915. The work to which he had devoted his life represented an achievement unprecedented in the history of publishing anywhere in the world. The Dictionary had taken its place as the ultimate authority on the language. It was first published in 1884.[2]

In 1857, at the suggestion of the dean of Westminster, Richard Chenevix Trench, the Philological Society resolved to prepare a large dictionary of the English language, intending to include as comprehensive a collection as possible of English words and meanings that had survived the Norman conquest or been introduced into the language after the conquest. The hope was that the final product, 'by the completeness of its vocabulary, and by the application of the historical method to the life and use of words, might be worthy of the English language and of English scholarship'[3.] There were three standard dictionaries of the time, those of Charles Richardson, Noah Webster, and Joseph Worcester. The proposed new one was to be based on historical principles: that is, each word and meaning was to be supported by evidence drawn from works of every kind—those of famous authors, such as Chaucer, Malory, Shakespeare, Milton, Pope, Wordsworth, and Dickens, but also those of 'minor' authors, private letters, glossaries and early dictionaries, technical handbooks, newspapers, learned journals, and so on.

Herbert Coleridge was appointed editor, and as a first step he established an ambitious reading programme in which quotational evidence was to be systematically gathered. Several hundred readers were drawn into the scheme, including Thomas Brushfield, F. J. Furnivall, the novelist Charlotte Yonge, and the etymologist Professor W. W. Skeat. One of the odder incidents in the history of the dictionary was that a particularly prolific contributor of illustrative quotations, Dr W. C. Minor, was later discovered to have been confined in the Broadmoor Asylum for the Criminally Insane during the time of his contributions—he had shot and killed a man some years before in an apparently motiveless attack. Minor provided an invaluable service to the dictionary with his painstaking lexicographical research.

The importance of these readers to the larger project cannot be overemphasized. One reader (Thomas Austin) had produced 165,000 supporting quotations by the time that the first volume (A–B) was published in 1888. Brushfield suggested 72,000 of which 50,000 were accepted for publication. Furnivall had produced 30,000 in the same period, and Minor came up with between 5000 and 8000 quotations. Ultimately, the dictionary was very much a collaborative effort. Other assistants, including members of Murray's own family, helped with sorting and filing the material as it arrived. About fifty names, including those of Dr Brushfield, Charlotte Yonge and W. W. Skeat, are listed in the preface to volume 1 as having sub-edited, or prepared for sub-editing, the quotational evidence submitted to the editor.

However successful the reading of sources was to become, in the early years of the project it proved inadequate. What Dean Trench had grandly described in 1857 as 'this drawing as with a sweep-net over the whole extent of English literature' had by 1860 garnered only about one-tenth of the quotations that were ultimately needed. In 1861 Herbert Coleridge died. Furnivall was persuaded to take on the editorship, but his methods of work were erratic and in the end unsuccessful. As a first step he proposed the compilation of a concise dictionary, and forecast that such a book could be produced in three years. Both ideas came to nothing. Negotiations with Macmillan as possible publisher of the society's dictionary also proved to be unfruitful, and the dictionary's future was uncertain.

In March 1879, after a series of prolonged discussions, the Philological Society came to an agreement with the Oxford University Press concerning the editing and publication of what was now to be known as The Oxford English Dictionary (OED). After consulting several scholars, among them Frederick Furnivall, Henry Sweet, and the comparative philologist Max Müller, the delegates of the press offered the task of editing the dictionary to James Murray. He was invited to edit the material for publication in parts. It was proposed that he would be able to compile the successive fascicles with help from a small editorial staff while he was still teaching at Mill Hill School. Murray, estimating that the dictionary could be finished in ten years in an estimated 7000 pages, accepted.

In 1885 the second part (Ant–Batten) of the dictionary was published. Murray left Mill Hill and moved with his family to Oxford, where he could devote his whole time to the dictionary. He worked, with a small group of modestly paid assistants, in a new scriptorium built for the purpose in the garden of his house at 78 Banbury Road. Three more editors joined him.

Henry Bradley was his second independent editor, beginning in 1889. He and his assistants had a separate office in Broad Street, Oxford.

By the end of his career Brushfield had contributed 72,000 slips of which 50,000 were accepted for publication. Only two others contributed as many[2].

Hannah and Thomas had now completed their family. Sydney Francis, born in 1866, was followed by Edith Sarah in 1867. Archibald was born in 1870 and Eleanor Miller in 1874 in Whitechapel. Helena was the last of the children born in 1876. Meanwhile Thomas N Brushfield was at school in Guildford from where he went up to Trinity College, Cambridge in 1876, eventually to qualify as a doctor in 1884 and then to specialize in the treatment of lunacy just as his father had thirty years before. The younger Dr Thomas, though perhaps not as brilliant as his father, was well known as the discoverer of "Brushfield spots" in children and the condition was named after him.

Thomas Brushfield, father of Thomas and Richard, born in 1798 in Ashford, Derbyshire died on 1 September 1875 and was buried beside his wife, Susan. He had lived in Church Street, Spitalfields for most of his life. His will was witnessed by both sons on 30 September and the value proven was just under £50,000 - a considerable fortune in those days.

Richard Brushfield, still an 'oil and colourman' man in the firm his father founded, married Esther Payne in 1867. He was then living in Lewisham.

Thomas and Hannah had buried their daughter Florence Elizabeth, born in 1862, at the early age of 19 in 1881. The two years 1881 and 1882 were miserable ones indeed for the family.

Dr Brushfield's chief medical works were Medical Certificates of Insanity which appeared in the Lancet in 1880 and Some Practical Hints on Symptoms, Treatments, and Medico-Legal Aspects of Insanity, a paper read before the Chester Medical Society in 1890. In these he laid out the shortcomings of the system of patient commitment into secure accommodation. Much of his advice found its way into legislation eventually. In the treatment of the insane he endevoured to explain that many of the procedures in use, when he started in Bedlam in 1852, were not only unsuitable but dangerous. The range of drugs at his disposal for the control of the insane were not available then or at all during his lifetime. However, by persuasion, he brought about what amounts to a revolution in the management of asylums.

His forced retirement came as a huge disappointment to friends and colleagues in Woking. He was honoured by several presentations and departed for Budleigh Salterton with their applause and thanks ringing in his ears.

Budleigh Salterton and East Budleigh

The coastline forms the western most section of Jurassic coast, and the cliffs on either side of the town are the unique Red Devonian Sandstone. The beach, which is formed of large pebbles, extends for 2.5 miles, from Littleham Cove to the west, to Otterhead in the east, where the River Otter meets the sea.

Historically it formed part of East Budleigh Hundred. It falls within Aylesbere Deanery for ecclesiastical purposes. The population was 1014 in 1801 2653 in 1901 4725 in 1991. Separated from East Budleigh in 1894.

Chapter 9

1882

Budleigh Salterton, Devon

In those days the small village of East Budleigh was both larger and more interesting than its near neighbour Budleigh Salterton, with much more history and, important to Thomas Brushfield, with a fine and ancient All Saints Church. He was, just as his father before him, a convinced churchman and was determined to play a full part in church life.

However, the house he found to suit his purpose, was situated close to the sea in Budleigh Salterton. It was a run-down early Victorian villa with a garden full of weeds and really much too small for purpose. He bought the house and added an extension to the north and north-west with rounded walls and some striking stained glass windows. It was refurbished and fitted out as a library by the Salterton builder William Keslake. The library eventually contained about 10,000 volumes and was the largest privately owned collection in the West Country with a number of valuable items.

It is easy to see why Thomas and his small family chose Budleigh as the place to settle. The small village was conveniently situated near to the city of Exeter where there were rapidly improving communications to all parts of the country and Thomas was determined to keep in touch with his many friends in Woking and in Chester.

But there were other reasons that he and Hannah had in moving to East Devon in preference to the many other possible south coast towns. Thomas was now finished with his professional life and wanted to indulge his second life as an author, a bibliophile and as a researcher into historic literary fields that presented an interest and challenge. The decision was driven by the area's strong association with Sir Walter Ralegh. Thomas is recorded as having a firm view about Sir Walter's name. He maintained that Sir Walter did not use the Raleigh spelling we often see today and so he also refused to use it.

Sir Walter Ralegh was an explorer, soldier and writer who was imprisoned in the Tower of London and eventually put to death after being accused of treason by James I. Before serving in the Huguenot army in France he studied at Oxford, and became a favorite of Queen Elizabeth after serving in her army in Ireland. He was knighted in 1585, and within two years became captain of the queen's guard. Between 1584 and 1589 he established a colony near Roanoke Island, which he named Virginia. Much of his writings and poetry from this time were destroyed.

East Budleigh will for ever be associated with Ralegh. He was born in Hayes Barton just outside the village in a fine Elizabethan farmhouse that can be viewed in a heavily restored but recognizable condition as a fine fully thatched and listed farmhouse with an E shaped plan of traditional Elizabethan design. All Saints Church is associated with both Ralegh and Drake and there still exist bench ends to show these connections. But the finest house associated with Ralegh is undoubtedly the splendid Vicar's Mead in the village centre near to the Sir Walter Raleigh (sic) public house. Though Vicar's Mead is not now often open to the public it contains many original features and Raleghana (Brushfield's name for his studies) including diamond-scratched-marks on the window panes. Vicar's Mead is believed to be the Ralegh schoolroom.

There is a poignant story about Ralegh told in the village records. Sir Walter led a charmed and successful life as both naval hero and buccaneer and this made him a wealthy man. He fell foul of King James I though, who ordered his re-arrest in Plymouth following his last fateful and unsuccessfully voyage in search of Spanish treasure. After his arrest he was taken to the Tower of London to meet his executioner. He passed though East Budleigh on his way to meet the executioner's axe at Westminster and paused there to remember the old and better days.[1]

Historically associated with East Budleigh, Sir Walter was also one of the remarkable poets and authors of his day and this was the main attraction for Thomas Brushfield. As has been observed, there is always room for another biography of Ralegh. Brushfield had decided to make his life's work a study of every aspect of Ralegh's writings and to bring his scholar's mind to the solution of the many conundrums he had observed related to Ralegh's work.

Thomas and Hannah, with daughter Edith, came to live in Budleigh Salterton in 1882 in the house called The Cliff situated exactly opposite the house occupied by Adolphus Trollope and his wife, Fanny, some 10 years earlier. Adolphus was the elder brother of the better known Anthony Trollope who was by then working for the Post Office in Ireland. Thomas Brushfield was able to purchase Adolphus' desk when he moved in. It became a prized possession of later generations.

The Cliff was small and run-down so Thomas set about improving and repairing it. The main feature of the improvement was to be the splendid library set out to the north of the house resplendent with stained glass windows and with bespoke book shelves made by the local firm of Keslake. When the family was installed he had room for his collection of 10,000 books, many of them associated with his study of the life of Ralegh.

Another reason why Thomas chose Budleigh as the favoured place in which to retire is given by his friend Dr Moreton

One of his former house surgeons at Chester Asylum - Dr Walker - was established there in practice. An intimate friendship between these old colleagues, which continued up to the death of Dr Brushfield, helped both of them, in many directions, towards the sanitary conditions of the place, as well as materially assisting in the measures for recreation and amusement.

The first of these projects was the establishment and management of the Budleigh Salterton Cottage Hospital which opened in 1888 as a result of public subscription.

From its beginnings in March of that year, when it started life "for the benefit of poor persons suffering from accident or non-infectious disease, who cannot be properly attended to in their own homes" the hospital has always been enthusiastically supported as one of the town's good causes. One of the earliest benefactors was the Reverend James Boucher, who donated £525 to the building fund to help launch the project. The nearby Boucher Way is named after him. Originally there was accommodation for six patients, even eight in an emergency, though the hospital grew steadily in size and the provision of treatment over the years. Most of the funds were found

The Railway in Budleigh Salterton

Locally sponsored, mainly as a result of Brushfield's lobbying, led to the line being opened as far as Budleigh Salterton on 15 May 1897 with one intermediate stop at East Budleigh and a second being opened in 1899 at Newton Poppleford. Although privately owned the line was extended in 1903 by the London and South Western Railway to Exmouth via Littleham. Major reduction in the services along the line in the 1960s led to a corresponding decrease in usage. The line closed to freight traffic on 27 January 1964 and to passengers on 6 March 1967.

by the Honorable Mark Rolle, local landowner and benefactor.

The hospital still flourishes to this day albeit in a somewhat different guise in its NHS manifestation. In 2009 when Dr Evans presided at a Friends' garden party:

Budleigh Salterton Hospital's League of Friends will be celebrating the completion of building and improvement projects totaling £262,000 when they hold their annual garden party on Saturday 1 August. The Arcadia Jazz Band will be in attendance.

The original subscription list was opened with the aim of

completion as a memorial to Queen Victoria's First Jubilee.

......everybody gave as liberally as everyone could, and
without a single objection - this, aided by the munificence of
the late Rev. Mr Boucher, Vicar of Littleham, an old resident of
Budleigh Salterton, allowed the present institution to be built
and started.

Dr Brushfield was the chairman of the committee for quite 20
years; Dr Walker and Dr Evans were the surgeons and on Dr
Walker's retirement, Dr Semple took his place.
Dr Moreton says:

The hospital has done and is doing good work in the
pleasantest manner possible, and under the present matron,
Miss Lewis, the patients are most kindly and tenderly looked
after. Beyond this, owing to the thoughtfulness of many
residents in sending fish, meat, vegetables, fruit and flowers,
the necessary yearly expenses are very modest.

There were many other projects to keep Brushfield and Walker
busy. One of them was the provision of the town's water supply.
Others related to the various clubs and societies. More of these later
but as for Thomas' own special interests Dr Moreton observes:

In every direction - amateur theatricals, readings, penny
and otherwise, lectures on a variety of subjects, soirees, and
now and then quite ambitious concerts - all found an ample
store and resource in the always acceptable, mostly humorous

ability of Dr Brushfield, accompanied as he occasionally was, by his eldest daughter, Mrs Shepherd, a most delightful pianist.

Deep sea fishing was a popular pursuit in East Devon much followed by Thomas Brushfield. The brothers Middleton were his boatmen who arranged his fishing trips. It is remembered that he was always most generous with the distribution of his catch.[2]

Now his already phenominal range of interests was extended even futher to sporting activies.

Croquet

Croquet is a satisfying sport utilising tactics and touch in equal measure. It combines strategy and precison and is a bit like snooker on grass or a combination of chess and golf. Croquet can be enjoyed by all ages and sexes on an equal basis.

The origin of croquet, like that of many other sports, is obscure. Although the game has been played in roughly its present form for about one hundred years, its antecedents extend back many centuries. As long ago as the fourteenth century, peasants in Brittany and Southern France amused themselves playing a game called Paille Maille, in which crude mallets were used to knock balls through hoops made of bent willow branches. This ancestral version of croquet persisted, and by the seventeenth century, Pele Mele, as it was called in England, had become popular with Charles II and his court. Diarist Samuel Pepys, in his entry of April 2, 1661, wrote that "I went into St. James Parke, where I saw the Duke of Yorke playing at Pesle Mesle - the first time that I ever saw that sport."

Chapter 10

1882

Croquet and Community

One of Thomas Brushfield's new interests was the croquet club perched on top of the hill overlooking the town. In 1892 he became secretary to the club and in 1896 its president. In those days the social interests of the town's smart set dictated that membership was *de rigeur*.

One could join the Archery and Croquet Club (probably founded before 1868 though certainly in full swing for croquet by 1872), located on the plateau at the top of the hill opposite the cricket ground where, for the sum of 10/- annually one might enjoy both archery and croquet and the very new sport of lawn tennis (named sphairistike by its inventor), which largely replaced Battledor and Shuttlecock as an outdoor sport.

The influential landowner in East Devon was the Hon. Mark Rolle, eldest son of Lord Clinton, who let two fields of 3 acres to Mr Harwood who in turn let them to the club for the sum of £4 annually. By 1872 the club rented the fields directly from the Rolle Estate whilst Mr Harwood was given the tenancy of Frogmore Meadow in East Budleigh in exchange. The Hon. Mark Rolle also presented building materials worth £12 to the club so that by 1870 there was also a pavilion or shelter measuring 20 ft by 5 ft. Croquet requires a court equal to two tennis courts so, taken together with the archery ground, full use was made of all 3 acres.

The entrance to the club was in Cricket Field Lane opposite the Cricket Club (now the Games Club). By 1878 the first of three tennis courts were established. There was also croquet and a photograph of 1879, with General Goodwin in front - later a friend and collaborator of Thomas Brushfield - which shows a group standing beside a croquet court equipped with the standard round-topped hoops of the time. The General lived in Stoneborough Lodge nearby.

In April 1884 the club already had a groundsman, Matthew Davey, who for 2/6 for each working day became "caretaker of the grounds". Dr Brushfield, then secretary, engaged him to serve the "Budleigh Salterton Archery, Croquet and Lawn Tennis Club", as it was then known. Much of the improvements to the club were made as a direct result of Dr Brushfield's enthusiastic participation in meetings and planning.

Budleigh is known for the number of successful men and women who have come to live in the town after their hard-working careers have ended. They soon banded into interest groups such as the croquet club, the hospital, the cricket club (another particular favourite of Thomas Brushfield) and the football club. There is now a flourishing golf course and that, too, would undoubtedly have attracted the interest of Brushfield had it happened in his time.

The leading light in the archery and croquet club when Brushfield arrived in 1882 was General J E Goodwin who was its celebrated president. R W Friend later became secretary after leaving a senior civil service appointment to retire to the town. Dr Walker was a leading member as was R Lipscombe the long-serving steward of the Rolle Estates. General Goodwin, who had commanded the 41st Regiment of Foot was a much-decorated and heroic figure who had survived campaigns in the Crimea and India. He had served in the relief of Sebastopol and in many other actions. The social life of the rapidly growing town of Budleigh Salterton revolved around the croquet club.

The first reference to the tennis tournament, arranged by Brushfield, occurs in a letter dated 8th September 1884 from Lipscombe to Dr. Brushfield about subscriptions to the tournament. to say that the prizes had been carried off by visitors "....which was a very good advertisement for the place....". Mr Lipscomb was indeed a most excellent contact. General Goodwyn C.B., president in 1885, had a committee of 8 men and 9 ladies. The accounts of the year showed income of £43 and a surplus of £9 that was earmarked for a new mower. The income included £1-10-0 for winter grazing which was the way the courts were cut in winter. In 1887 bowls was added as an additional sport.

Dr Brushfield then succeeded General Goodwin as president. The record for 1888 shows that smoking was not allowed in or near the pavilion. No children under 14 could become members and, indeed, were not allowed in the grounds at all unless accompanied by an adult. Dogs were not allowed in the grounds on pain of a 1/- fine for the first offence and 2/- thereafter. There was an archery secretary and Mondays were the important days since only scores achieved and recorded on a Monday qualified for archery prizes. Tennis players provided their own "bats" and balls, croquet players their own mallets but bowlers enjoyed the use of club woods. Not very family friendly, then, though Brushfield was a family man. Obviously there was no prejudice against women who enjoyed equal status on the committee.

The Railway came to Budleigh Salterton in 1897 and this dramatically increased the attraction of the town to both visitors and residents. The influx of retired people from London then started in earnest. Dr Brushfield was a director of the railway company and influential in arguing for its extension to Budleigh.

At the AGM of the croquet club in 1889, chaired by Dr Brushfield, it was proposed to plan a new "£100 pavilion". This was presumably a standard article, which cost £50 to erect. Members, led by him, set about raising the funds. To this end he organised, produced and acted in two plays put on in the town's Public Rooms one entitled "Alone" and another "Area Belle" which raised £10 towards the target. This made possible the pavilion to be built at a cost of £66-8-0 though materials were once again supplied at the expense of Mark Rolle.

Home rule was the political topic of the time when, in 1893, the club's main activity was the new and rapidly growing sport of lawn tennis. This sport became the new interest of Thomas Brushfield who was also now prominent in the orgainsation of the cricket club. There was now a new groundsman, Staddon, who was paid the sum of 18/- per week. As a concession he was allowed to use the horse, cart and horse-mower to cut and roll the cricket field provided he completed this before breakfast.

By May 1896, there were three full croquet courts and five tennis courts. Outdoor badminton had fizzled out and archery had probably ceased. The first open croquet tournament took place and was a great success. It was one of the first open croquet tournaments held anywhere in the country. Appropriately it was won by Mrs T.C.G.Evans who was the player to beat in those days and she received a small broach-like shield to mark the occasion. As a result of Thomas Brushfield's meticulous chasing, to coincide with the Queen's Diamond Jubilee on June 22 in 1897, the railway came to

Budleigh Salterton from Tipton St. John and the population of the town rejoiced greatly. The club held a bicycle gymkhana and raised £16. Stadden looked after the pony that pulled the court mower and cart. His harness cost £3-12-0 and his food for the year cost 16/6. The railway made Budleigh Salterton easy to get to, though the link with Exmouth was still some years away.

Dr Brushfield was still much concerned with the croquet club in 1904 when a new pony arrived. Caretaker of the grounds, Gosling, was replaced by Walley who came for 18/- per week. Palmers, the builders, made many useful additions to the changing rooms and lavatories siting the new buildings close to the entrance to the club in Cricket Field Lane. All this work was paid for by the Hon. Mark Rolle. Walley departed and was replaced by Creasey. The Hon. Mark Rolle gave £60 towards the new building work. Tea was served on every day in the summer.

But Thomas' keenest recreation, one of which he availed himself every day and mostly all day, was in his library.

Dr Moreton :

> Before breakfast he was at (his books), and from Breakfast to lunch with very few exceptions, something in hand to be done. It was always work of some sort, but there was so much of love in it that it really did not look like work.

More of his antiquarian interest later; in 1883 he joined the Devonshire Association and for over 20 years he contributed papers and articles to the annual transactions of the society on a number of subjects relating to the county. In 1893 he was elected president for the meeting held in Torquay. His presidential address on the

Literature of Devonshire up to the year 1640 ran to 125 pages and was an exhaustive list of everything published in hte county up to that date.

Dr Brushfield was a committed churchman and his interest was immediately drawn to the church in East Budleigh, All Saints. He worshipped at the church and participated fully in church life. His definitive work describing All Saints Church, published in two volumes may still be obtained at reputable booksellers. His publication The Accounts of a Churchwarden is a most readable and detailed account of church life over the centuries.

When Thomas Brushfield first came to Budleigh Salterton in 1882 the village was much smaller than East Budleigh. In fact if one spoke of Budleigh it was taken for granted that one meant East Budleigh. Budleigh Salterton (or just plain Salterton) was a small collection of houses a mile or so away beside the sea. In the 1880s there were 3400 residents in total in both places. By contrast in 2011 there were 6500 inhabitants of Budleigh Salterton and a mere 900 in East Budleigh.

In Dr Brushfield's day East Budleigh was the place to attend church though a small chapel at ease had been established for some time in Upper East Terrace. Now that Salterton was growing so quickly it was time things changed and, with typical enthusiasm and drive, Thomas set about the establishment of a new Church on land just behind the main street.

Meanwhile, in 1990 the Chester Medical Society unanimously elected him as an honorary member and he was a frequent visitor at their annual gatherings and dinners.

Dr Thomas Nadauld Brushfield died in 1910 due to a chill contracted on his return home from Buxton and it may truly be said that not only the inhabitants of Budleigh Salterton, but those of the whole of Devon are in every way the poorer for his death.

St Peter's Church

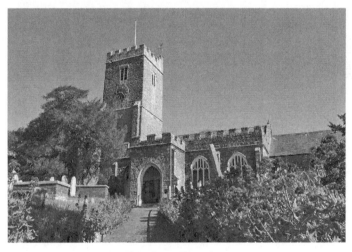

All Saints Church

Chapter 11

1883

Vestryman

Like his father before him Thomas Brushfield was a committed Christian and supporter of his church. This he showed in both Chester and Woking whenever the call of his professional work allowed.

When he moved to Budleigh Salterton in 1882 he was faced with a dychotomy. Because the communities had grown at such different rates it was the smaller East Budleigh that was regarded as the parish and in the now much larger Budleigh Salterton only a small chapel at ease existed since 1852. For this reason Thomas decided to make All Saints Church in East Budleigh his spiritual home.

As usual he threw himself into his new interest and became a solid supporter of the church that overlooked the fields and cottages of the picturesque village. Though this was not the church where Ralegh was christened (that was supposed to be Place, in Colleton Raleigh) it had many Ralegh associations and a fine set of pews with interesting carved bench ends full of historical reference[1].

Now in 1805 Brushfield commenced a work similar to the archaeological work he had been drawn to in Chester. Having an ordered mind and the capacity for hours of investigative work he set out to write a description in the minutest detail of the church and the stories that surrounded it. Using his tried and tested method of working he commenced the considerable task[2].

As the manuscripts left to us show he used a particular method of work for all his lengthy projects. First he had a number of blank books bound with paper of good quality into which he would enter his fair copy. This might consist of lists, paragraphs and cuttings from books, letters, published material or periodicals that came to hand. Mostly he found materials in the form of text and diagrams in the periodicals of the day and to this end he built a collection of editions of the *Gentleman's Magazine.* A considerable part of his library was given over to texts of this type. He would carefully cut out the relevant text using a razor and then paste it into the book he was creating.

But, perhaps because of his competence and training as an anatomist, Brushfield skillfully sketched what he observed and his work is peppered with illustrative drawings of the most detailed nature. No doubt this made for difficulties when it came to revising the work later.

He had a method of arranging his work that possibly harkened back to his early medical training. When his library was broken up soon after his death some fifty commonplace books were discovered amongst his effects. In these he would plan his day and week in great detail by splitting the tasks he had set into as many tiny sections as seemed appropriate. Using the current commonplace book, usually in the form of a readily available exercise bookcopy , he would lay out his work and then tick off each one as it was pasted or written into the final volume. No tick appeared unless he had traced the source required and made a draft of the paragraphs to be entered. His handwriting was tiny though precise and readable.

When he was satisfied with the text and illustrations in the final copy the bound manuscript book would be sent to Henry Commins his chosen printer in Exeter. Commins, having set the text would provide the proofs to Brushfield for reading and correction. In its final form the corrected proofs were set and published. This process was time-consuming; rarely did the work emerge in less than three and sometime even five years. Brushfield complained in 1908 that his eyesight at his age now of 80 was so poor that he could no longer undertake the proof reading or detailed correction. This then passed to Commins' son who was warmly congratulated by Brushfield on his work.

Dr Brushfield's work in relation to the East Budleigh parish and church started with his detailed *Notes on the Parish of East Budleigh* (published 1890). In this he gathered many historic facts that reveal how the church worked in relation to its parishioners rich and poor and how the vicar went about his work.

It was not until *The Church of All Saints, East Budleigh Parts I -III (1891, 1892, 1894)* was produced that his powers of description and and precision of the archaeologist's method of working were fully evident. He leaves nothing of any minute importance to the imagination. His sketches are superb and the hitherto undiscovered architectural detail makes excellent reading.

The work did not end there. He trolled through all the texts he could unearth from vestry papers and archives throughout this corner of East Devon and found items from church accounts that illustrate the importance attached by every parish to making a proper statement of the expenses that were incurred down to the last farthing. This resulted in *The Churchwarden's Accounts of East Budleigh (1894)*. In this transcription of the copperplate handwritten ledgers Brushfield revealed that he had a rare insight into the things that were of importance in those long-forgotten days[3].

By 1890 it was becoming obvious that the spiritual needs of the much enlarged small town of Budleigh Salterton were being ignored. There was pressure from the growing community for change.

Thomas Brushfield had by now eight years of experience of retirement in East Devon. He had made many friends. There was the redoubtable General Goodwin with his memories of battles long ago and the aptly named Robert Friend who lived in Kersbrook and who had now grown close to him. There was the very useful Robert Lipscomb who had the ear of the most important land owner in Devon. Then there was his old friend Dr Walker who had been a and valued colleague for so many years who may have been the original reason for his decision to come to Budleigh in the first place. Then there were Carmichael and Ravenscroft both of whom he had met and joined at the croquet club. Most of all in this context there was the Rev. James Boucher, vicar of Littleham near Exmouth, who had been so helpful when the cottage hospital was planned. They jointly approached architect Mr George Fellowes-Prynne of Queen's Gate, Westminster, who designed an elegant church to seat 640 people with 34 others in the main part of the church and a further 34 in the chancel. At this time the population of the town was 1770 as measured in the 1881 census. A cost of between £6,890 and £9,970 was expected and the work went to Luscombs of Exeter. The *Church in the West* of 29th April 1893 reported:

> The foundation stone was laid by Miss Rolle and since
> then the work has gone on steadily.... A greater contrast to the
> old unsightly chapel of Holy Trinity could scarcely be
> imagined... The tower and spire which will reach a height of
> 140 feet are not yet erected... Externally, with its red tiled

roofs, Devon Limestone and marble facings and dressings of Doulting stone, the appearance of the building ... is extremely picturesque. It will look even better when the lofty tower and spire are erected.

In the parish magazine of May 1893:

Quite early in Tuesday morning (25th April 1893) Budleigh Salterton was full of life and brightness as the bishop of Exeter, Dr Bickersteth, preached the sermon.

Dr Brushfield joined the bishop and Mark Rolle in the place of honour at the celebratory luncheon, with the rural dean, the vicar of East Budleigh, Mr Baker and Mr Prynne. But it was to be another seven years before the status of a district chapelry was assigned to St Peter's.

Sadly, in so many people's opinion, then and now, the church was left without its tower and steeple, which materially affected much of its planned majestic aspect. The full sum required to fund the building of the church had been subscribed by Mark Rolle out of personal raher than Rolle estate funds but a decision was reached to spend the remainder upon a new chapel to serve the growing population in Knowle, a village just to the north of Budleigh.

Dr Brushfield could now worship at St Peter's Church just a stroll away from his home. The St Peter's burial ground was the place chosen at his wish for his interment in 1911.

There were many Brushfield works, papers and books that dealt with his church interests. Amonst these were *The Bishopric of Exeter, 1419 - 20: a Contribution to the History of the See* and diverse papers*: The Destruction of Vermin in Rural Parishes(1897); John Sixtinus, Archpriest of Haccombe, sixteenth Century (1902); Aids to the Poor in a Rural Parish (1889);* all of which were stimulated by his time as church warden in All Saints, East Budleigh and his researches into nearby parishes.

Exeter newspapers

It was Sam Farley, an established printer, who started the first weekly newspaper, the Exeter Postman, in the city, perhaps as early as 1704; his paper may have been the first outside of London and was certainly the third. The first newspaper personality in the city was **Andrew Brice** who was involved in publishing newspapers from before 1715 until his death in 1773; he personified the best of early journalism and in 1727 reported on corruption in St Thomas' debtors prison, ironically spending time in 1730 confined to his house for not paying his fine for the libel alleged on the gaoler in the prison.

Robert Trewman's Exeter Mercury or West Country Advertiser of 1763 would evolve into Trewman's Exeter Flying Post by 1770, and become the first, long lived Exeter newspaper of any substance. It was published throughout the 19th century, reporting local and national news to an increasingly literate population. By the early 19th century it was firmly established at 225/226 High Street, an address that would become synonymous with newspaper publishing in Exeter. Its rivalry with Thomas Latimer's Western Times, published from Fore Street would galvanise public opinion for reform and better conditions, throughout Victoria's reign.

Chapter 12

1854 - 1910

Antiquary

During his professional life, from 1850 to 1882, Dr Brushfield had little opportunity to undertake the demanding tasks of both literary research and publication of the results. During this period the few works to appear related to the subject of the treatment of lunatics 1880 when he published a paper in the Lancet entitled *Certificates of Insanity*. He also wrote a paper and read it before the Chester Medical Society in 1890 *Some Practical Hints on Symptoms, Treatments, and Medico-Legal Aspects of Insanity*. Other than these there were no other papers or larger works published or prepared before 1882, the year in which he retired to Budleigh.

Then he joined the Devonshire Association and scarely a year passed without one or more papers from his pen appearing in the annual proceedings. He was also a frequent contributor to *the Western Antiquary, Devon Notes and Queries*, and other kindred publications.

The volume and range of his contributions printed in the Transactions of the association are impressive. Here is the list:

A Bibliography of the Rev. George Oliver, D.D., of Exeter

The Rev'd George Oliver DD, (1781-1867), was born at Newington, Surrey, 1782, and came to Exeter in 1807 remaining in the City until his death in 1861. He was an ordained Roman Catholic priest. Doctor Oliver was well known as a laborious antiquary (which is almost certainly what commended a study of him to Brushfield) and his works on ecclesiastical antiquities in Devon earned him a high reputation for scholarship. He is known to have published at least 27 papers. In this paper Brushfield lists the publications in Dr Oliver's name.

(1888)

The Bishopric of Exeter, 1419 - 20: a Contribution to the History of the See, (1888)

Widely quoted listing of bishops and their literary achievements.

(1888)

Andrew Brice[1] and the Early Exeter Newspaper Press

The character of Andrew Brice, although very pronounced, is by no means an easy one to estimate or to describe. His natural good abilities, aided by a good education, placed him in a position far above his compeers, and understandibly Polwhele's remark on the Parleys being 'no match for the learning and abilities of Brice.' That he possessed literary talents of a high order is shown by his article on Exeter in his *Gazetteer.* Of another order of composition, and as displaying his versatility in a praiseworthy direction, some of his newspaper articles may be mentioned. But, on the other hand, when excited by political animosity or by private enmity, he appears to have thrown off all restraint and as he was a master in the arts of vituperation, satire, and unscrupulous sneering, and coarse in his statements, we are not surprised to learn that he was constantly embroiled in literary and even in more active warfare.

He was vigorous and thorough in all that he did; a model of

plodding perseverance, as the circumstances of his early life have already demonstrated, a man of strong feelings and powerful resentment. Testy, painfully sensitive, never forgetting or forgiving an injury, and governed by strong impulses, whether for good or for evil. And yet, like those of a large class, his faults were far more patent to the world than were his virtues. His character was antithetic, powerful in extremes. Although a good fighter, even when on the losing side, he often acknowledged himself to be in the wrong. In his daily life no one was kinder, displayed more hospitality, or was more charitable all these good qualities were especially exhibited to his poorer relatives, as well as to the 'poor players.' Of him Dr. Oliver reports 'that he was a great favourite with his brother Exonians; he ... was frank, humorous, and independent.' He calls him 'facetious,' a point of character on which Andrew appeared to pride himself, as he sometimes dubbed himself 'Merry Andrew,' at other times 'Andrew, surnamed Merry.' He certainly possessed strong individuality, and was eccentric in speech, in manner, and dress. (1888)[2]

For further notes on the life of Andrew Brice, see below.

Who Wrote the "Exmoor Scolding and Courtship"?

Supplementary to the Andrew Brice publication of 1888, remarks on the early history of the Exeter newspaper press, with a supplementary article on the authorship of the "Exmoor scolding and courtship."

(1888)

The Literature of Devon up to the year 1640

Dr Brushfield's presidential address to the Devonshire Association annual general meeting at Torquay. Generally recognised as a literary *tour de force* in which he includes every known Devon literary source from the middle of the 11th century up to 1640.

(1893)

Richard Izaclee and his "Antiquities of Exeter"
Extracts from a volume in Dr Brushfield's possession.

(1893)

Devonshire Briefs, Parts I and II (1896)

Description of a Perforated Stone Implement Found in the Parish of East Budleigh *(1890)*

and with these were the works related to the surrounding parishes and churches mentioned in the last chapter.

The Financial Diary of a Citizen of Exeter, 1631 - 43 (1901)
Brushfield discovered the manuscript and transcribed this work that details life in Exeter in the seventheenth century. The original is still to be seen in the Devon Heritage Centre following the break-up of Dr Brushfield's library in 1911[2]

The British Archaeological Association was *established in 1843 for the encouragement and prosecution of researches into the arts and monuments of the early and middle ages. A new series* VOL. VI.— 1900. was printed at the Bedford Press, London.

Dr Brushfield contributed papers to the Journal, any of the, dealing with subjects in Derbyshire. Brushfield's father came from

Ashford-by-the-Water and his mother, Susannah also came from the county. Dr Brushfield made a joint visit to the area for excavations with Thomas Bateman.

The papers read were:

On Norman Tympana, with especial reference to those of Derbyshire (1900)

After a visit to the church of Ashford-in-the-Water, using the Buxton Congress in 1899, for the purpose, inter alia, of inspecting the Norman tympanum preserved there, led to the suggestion that a Paper on the various tympana of that period still to be found in Derbyshire churches, might be acceptable to the members of this Association. An extract reads:

> It is known that many, perhaps the majority, of the principal doorways of the later Anglo-Saxon churches had semicircular heads, a feature continued into and to the end of the Norman period. It was, however, reserved for the architects of the twelfth century to fill up the space left between the arch and the square head of the door with a stone slab or **tympanum**. In many instances this was left quite plain, but the greater number were carved with devices extremely varied in character. Some bore patterns of geometric figures, chequers, etc. ; but the number of these were comparatively few, the majority being sculptured with representations of the human subject ; of animals, real or fabulous, with attendant scroll-work ; of scenes from Scripture, symbolical and real.

Derbyshire Funeral Garlands (1899)

(Read at the Buxton Congress, July 19th, 1899.)

Although mentioned by various writers, the first author to devote a special paper to the subject of Funeral Garlands was Mr. Ll. Jewitt, in one that appeared in the first number of the Reliquary, issued in 1860. Of this archaeological periodical he remained the editor from that year to the close of his life in 1886. Brushfield says:

> I may be permitted to add that I first called his attention to the garlands preserved in Ashford Church, during the period of a joint visit to the late Mr. Thomas Bateman, the well-known antiquary, of Lomberdale House, near Youlgreave.

Arbor Low (1899)

(Read at the Buxton Congress, July 20t/i, 1899.)

Situated on a long ridge of hill about one mile from Parsley Hay, south of a road leading from that place eastwards to YouWeave, three miles distant, and at an elevation of nearly 1,200 ft. above sea level, is a great prehistoric circle of earth and stone generally termed **Arbor Low**. It was first described by the Rev. S. Pegge (the Rector of Whittington) in a Paper read at a meeting of the Society of Antiquaries on May 29th, 1783, and printed in archaeologia, vii, 131-148, with a plate. Up to that period it was almost unknown, and received no mention from any writer ; nor is it entered in any of the county maps until after the publication of that Paper.

Brushfield adds:

> it is by far the most magnificent and capital Druidical remain of any we have in Derbyshire, not to say in all this part of England.

Ashford Church (1900)

Of particular interest for Brushfield and is a further exploration by him of the archaeology of Derbyshire.

Thomas Brushfield also contributed further papers to the Devonshire Association:

Britain's Burse or the New Exchange (1903)

James I suggested that there should be a new exchange called Britain's Burse, but the name did not catch on.[6]

Notes on the Punishment known as the "Drunkard's Cloak" of Newcastle -on-Tyne (1888)

Dr Brushfield had what can only be described as a morbid interest in punishments as laboriously he dissected various pamphlets and magazine articles and published works for the text cuttings that described the miseries suffered by unfortunates long ago.

William Andrews published, at the Hull Press, on August 11th, 1898, his work describing **Bygone Punishments**. He says:

About twenty–five years ago I commenced investigating the history of obsolete punishments, and the result of my studies first appeared in the newspapers and magazines. In 1881 was issued "Punishments in the Olden Time," and in 1890 was published "Old Time Punishments": both works were well received by the press and the public, quickly passing out of print, and are not now easily obtainable. I contributed in 1894 to the Rev. Canon Erskine Clarke's popular monthly, the Parish Magazine, a series of papers entitled "Public

Punishments of the Past."

In three bound manuscript volumes (Devon Studies Library) Brushfield set out his detailed descriptions of punishments meted out in past years. In this paper he uses material collected for the series culled from his own library.

Papers that Dr Brushfield contributed to the Chester Archaeology Society's Journal which dealt with the same interest were:

On Obsolete Punishments, with Particular Reference to those of Cheshire : Part I, The Brank, or Scold's Bridle (1858)

Part II, The Ducking Stool and Allied punishments(1886)

Both of these are complete with the author's own sketches and written in a hand that, though tiny, is still easily legible. His work was bound in 3 manuscript volumes.

The Rows of Chester (1893)

The Roman Remains of Chester, with a particular Description of those discovered in Bridge Street in July, 1863. This was amongst the first of Brushfield's papers presented whilst he was still at the Chester Asylum. It marks his quickening interest in practical archaeology.

The Salmon Clause in the Indentures of Apprentices (1896)

Brushfield writes in 1896:

As anyone interested in folk-lore is fully aware, assertions are frequently made of practices once current which have passed into oblivion in comparatively recent times, of whose origin and cessation nothing is known. Whether such statements are altogether true, or are wholly false ; whether they contain a substratum of truth sufficient to act as the matters of great uncertainty. They may ultimately be proved to be founded on fact, or to be entirely mythical, present evidence in either case being wanting.

These remarks are especially applicable to a belief, generally received as a truism throughout England, and by no means confined to it, that at one time Salmon was so exceedingly plentiful, that it was a common practice for the indentures of apprentices and agreements with servants to contain a clause, stipulating that they should not be required to partake of that fish for dinner more than a certain number of times weekly.

In his forensic manner Dr Brushfield sifts the evidence for what seemed to him to be a long-forgotten myth.

Brushfield's other archaeological works are:

Tideswell or Tidelow (Derbyshire Archaeological Society 1905)

A dissertation on the meaning of the place names.

Photograph of letter of Sir Walter Ralegh (Pros.,Soc. Antiquaries 1889)

The Origen of the Surname of Brushfield

("The Reliquary" 1886)

Obviously a subject of particular interest to Thomas, he looks at the literature, excavations and local stories. The surrounding area is part of the Chatsworth estate and so has Nadauld connotations.

Yew Trees in Churchyards "Antiquities and Curiosities of the Church" ed. by W Andrews, 1897)

A further inquiry into the contents of churches and churchyards around Budleigh.

As one of the principal readers for Dr Murray's New English Dictionary he contributed 72,000 references for that work, of which 50,000 were accepted, making him the third largest contributor.

Further details of the life of Andrew Brice[4]:

Andrew Brice was Exeter's first newspaper man of real significance; the son of a shoemaker, possibly born in Butchers Row in either 1790 or 1792, he claimed his father wanted him to become a minister, having a grammatical education in preparation, but he was in the event, too poor to fund him. The first Exeter newspaper, the Exeter Post-man appeared arguably in 1704 or more likely 1707. Within a short time other newspapers had appeared including Joseph Bliss's Exeter Post-Boy to which Brice was a printer's apprentice from the age of 17, but he 'roguishly absconded and deserted from my Service' in 1715, and hence, he was never made a freeman of the city. In 1717, he established his own newspaper, *The Exeter Postmaster* or the *Loyal Mercury* at the head of the Serge Market in Southgate-street (now renamed South Street). This was the first of a long series of titles published in Exeter including *Brice's Weekly journal*, from 1725, which are often referred to as ***Brice's Old Exeter Journal*** although the latter first appeared in 1746.

Like the 19th Century Thomas Latimer, Brice was outspoken, often getting into trouble for something he had published. Along with other newspaper editors, he was required to appear before Parliament for publishing their proceedings in 1718. He claimed he had merely passed on the contents of newsletters that were freely available at the coffee-houses of Exeter. Brice also like Latimer, was a crusader for the common folk of the city, including campaigning in 1727, for those who were thrown into the debtors prison at St Thomas, for which in 1730 he was fined for libel on the gaoler and, was himself, confined to his house for eight months for non-payment, spending his time writing a poem called Freedom. In addition, his mother and his wife died before he finally paid £103 for his freedom.

In July of 1830, Brice wrote of the earthquake or "violent concussion of the Earth" that hit Exeter. His description leaves nothing to the imagination:

"when of a sudden my Bed was forcibly agitated and shaken, as I may compare it, as a Bolting-Sieve or Searce is shov'd to and fro to sift your Flour , accompanied with a russling Noise, and Clashing of the Window. Which amazing mighty Shock continued, I believe, above Half a Minute, without Intermission."

He was a keen supporter of the early theatre in Exeter. When the Exeter players were persecuted during 1745, he published a poem defending them and attacking the Methodists, whom he named '*The Play-house Church*', or '*New Actors of Devotion.*' He also wrote prologues to plays which he often delivered himself, on the stage of the Seven Stars Inn.

By 1743, Andrew Brice, and his wife Sarah, were based at the sign of "The Printing Press" in Gandy Street. Not only did Brice work as a newspaper editor, but he devoted many years to his Grand gazetteer or Topographic Dictionary, a work of 1500 pages issued in 44 monthly parts in the years 1751 to 1755, and later in 1759 as a collected work. He covered a wide range of issues and wrote of the influence of education and "charity-school establishment whereby a hundred can read, write and cypher, now at this time, to ten that could barely read 50 or 60 years ago."

The Mobiad, or **Battle of the Voice** an Heroi-Comic Poem, Being a Description of an Exeter Election, written in 1738, was a satirical look at the mayoral elections of 1737 - publishing such a Hogarthian satire was dangerous at the time, which probably accounts for the delay in publication, until 1770. The work describes many places in the city including Castle Lane which he compares with Drury Lane in London or Damnation Alley in Plymouth. He also writes of Stepcote Hill:

A descent called Stepcote-Hill, to which the Butcherow leads.... the Guts, Blood, Litter, Ordure and a variety of Nastiness are, in hard showers of rain, rapidly carried.... into the River.

His Bricism style of satire, as it was called in 1781, used some creative language. Examples of his inventive vocabulary are : flim-sinewed, detorting, elboic, gloating, spuddling, plorant, spumiferous, vacive-noddle, cogitabundation, armipotence and scranch, all of which would keep an 18th century reader on his toes, never mind one from the 21st century.

In the **Mobiad**, Brice writes of his love for Exeter:

> Born, bred, brought up, and having always dwelt, in the City, I have a natural inclination to love her, as my mother, and wish sincerely for her welfare ... During my poor remains of life I shall heartily wish a continuance of prosperity, and growing reputation, in all respects, to this my beloved Exeter - from which no endeavours have prevail'd to draw me away.

He went into partnership with Barnabas Thorn in 1769 allowing Brice to go into semi-retirement before his death on 7th November 1773 at the age of 83. At the time of his death he was the oldest master mason and oldest master printer in England. Thorn continued running the newspaper, followed by his son Richard, until Richard's death in 1787.

In his **Grand Gazetteer,** Andrew Brice wrote that the Apollo Room at the New Inn was the only Lodge of Exeter Freemasons and it was appropriate that this former Master of the Lodge be layed out in the Apollo Room. The public were charged 1 shilling each to pay their respects, said to be an amount to help defer the cost of his funeral, Brice having hit hard times in his last years. From the Apollo Room, the remains of this past Master of the Lodge were accompanied by 200 of the fraternity of the Lodge of Exeter Freemasons, judges and several hundred citizens, to Bartholomew's Yard for interment in a grave without a headstone, and of unknown position. This epitaph was recorded by the contemporary historian,

Polwhele:

> Here lies Andrew Brice, the old Exeter printer
> Whose life lengthen'd out to the depth of its winter,
> Of his brethren masonic he took his last leave,
> Inviting them all to a lodge at his grave :
> Who, to shew their respect, and obedience, came   hither
> (Or rather the mob and the masons together)
> Sung a hymn to his praise, in a funeral tone,
> But disliking his lodging, return'd to their own.

This thorn in the side of the establishment was at last silenced, but his early influence upon journalism in Exeter would be continued by such as Robert Trewman and Thomas Latimer. The **Old Exeter Journal** was purchased in 1791 by **The Flying Post**'s Robert Trewman, a former apprentice of Brice, with his son, Richard Trewman establishing the **Flying Post** on the side of reform, a position that would have been applauded by Andrew Brice.

The Death of Sir Walter Ralegh

For a long time my course was a course of vanity. I have been a seafaring man, a soldier, and a courtier, and in the temptation of the least of these there is enough to overthrow a good mind and a good man. So I take my leave of you all, making my peace with God. I have a long journey to make and must bid the company farewell.

(Constance Fecher, The Last Elizabethan: A Portrait of Sir Walter Ralegh, page 230)

Then, in a loud voice, Sir Walter gave an order:

What do you fear? Strike, man, strike!

It is said that the blow fell - then fell again. There were tears in the eyes of the spectators, many of whom believed a just man had been unjustly killed on October 29, 1618. An unnamed poet, who watched the events, wrote this about what he had seen:

Great Heart! Who taught thee so to die?
Death yielding thee the Victory!
Where took'st thou leave of life? If here,
How could'st thou be so far from Fear? . . .
Farewell! Truth shall this story say,
We died: Thou only liv'st that Day.

Chapter 13

1882 - 1910

Brushfield's Raleghana

A Ralegh timeline[1]:

Date of Birth: Born in 1552

Place of Birth : Hayes Barton in Devonshire, England

Parents: Father - Walter Ralegh Mother: Katherine Gilbert (née Champernowne)

1552   Date of actual birth is unknown. He was initially educated in Vicar's Mead in East Budleigh

1567   The young Ralegh joined a troop of a hundred horse, raised by the Compte de Montgomerie

1572   August 24: He witnesses the St Bartholomew's Day massacre where French Protestants were massacred by French Catholics in Paris

1574   Attended Oriel College, Oxford

1575   Became a member of the Middle Temple

1578   Walter Ralegh sails with his half brother, Sir Humphrey Gilbert, to America

1579   Has an illegitimate daughter by Alice Goold, a local woman

1580   Ralegh helps to put down the Irish rebellion and becomes a favourite of Queen Elizabeth and becomes extremely wealthy from lucrative wine monopolies

1581   He founded the secret society called "The School of Night" which was closely related to the mysterious Rosicrucian movement

1584   Walter Ralegh receives the patent to explore and settle in North America. Walter Ralegh's fleet of seven vessels under Richard Grenville and Ralph Lane, with 108 men, reach Roanoke Island. Virginia colony of Roanoke Island established by Walter Ralegh

1585   January 6: Queen Elizabeth knights Walter Ralegh and makes him governor of the new territory discovered by Amadas and Barlowe. Ralegh names it "Virginia" in her honour

1586   Sir Francis Walsingham and Sir Walter Ralegh discover plot to assassinate Queen Elizabeth and replace her with Mary Queen of Scots (called the Babington Plot)

1587   Became captain of the Queen's guard.

1588   Ralegh donated "Ark Royal" to the English navy to lead the English fleet against the Spanish Armada. Sir Walter Ralegh was responsible for the joint defence of Devon and Cornwall against the expected Spanish invasion

1589   Sir Walter Ralegh & Sir Richard Grenville guard the sea approaches to Ireland

1592   Married Elizabeth (Bessie) Throckmorton incurring the wrath of Queen Elizabeth when she discovers that he has married her lady in waiting. Queen Elizabeth sends Sir Walter Ralegh to the Tower of London

He Is released when one of his ships brings back a huge treasure on the captured Spanish ship called the "Madre De Dios"

1593   Walter and Bessie have a son, also called Walter

1595   Sir Walter Ralegh leaves England to sail to the New World looking for the city of El Dorado. Sir Walter Ralegh fails to find the City of Gold but explores the Orinoco

1600   Appointment as governor of Jersey

1603   Queen Elizabeth I dies and is succeeded by King James, the son of Mary Queen of Scots King James, eager to make peace with the Spanish, imprisons him in the Tower of London on charges of treason

1604   Walter and Bessie have another son called Carew

1612   King James releases Ralegh, who promises to give King James a fortune if he allows him to return to Guiana

1616   He travels to Guiana but his mission fails and he attacks a Spanish settlement

1618   Sir Walter Ralegh is beheaded for attacking the Spanish Armada

Dr Brushfield's greatest literary achievement and probably the main reason he chose to come to East Devon for his retirement, were his researches into the works of Sir Thomas Ralegh. He possessed the most complete collection of Ralegh writings and publications outside the British and Bodleian Libraries.

Ralegh studied at Oxford before serving in the Huguenot army in France (1569). A rival of the Earl of Essex for the queen's favors, he served (1580) in Elizabeth's army in Ireland, distinguishing himself by his ruthlessness at the siege of Smerwick and by the plantation of English and Scots Protestants in Munster. Elizabeth rewarded him with a large estate in Ireland, knighted him (1585), and gave him trade privileges and the right to colonize America.

In 1587 he explored from North Carolina to present-day Florida, naming the region Virginia in honor of Elizabeth, the "Virgin

Queen." In 1587 Ralegh sent an ill-fated second expedition of colonists to Roanoke. In 1588 he took part in the victory over the Spanish Armada. He led other raids against Spanish possessions and returned with much booty. Ralegh forfeited Elizabeth's favor by his courtship of and subsequent marriage to one of her maids-of-honor, Bessy Throckmorton, and he was committed to the Tower (1592). Hoping, on his release, to recover his position, he led an abortive expedition to Guiana to search for El Dorado, a legendary land of gold. He helped to introduce the potato plant and tobacco use in England and Ireland.

Elizabeth's successor, James I, distrusted and feared Ralegh, charged him with treason and condemned him to death, but commuted the sentence to imprisonment in the Tower (1603). There Ralegh lived with his wife and servants, and wrote his History of the World (1614). He was released in 1616 to search for gold in South America. Against the king's undertaking to the Spanish, he invaded and pillaged Spanish territory, was forced to return to England without booty, and was arrested on the orders of the king. His original death sentence for treason was invoked, and he was executed at Westminster. A gifted poet, writer, and scholar, many of his poems and writings were destroyed. A pioneer of the Italian sonnet-form in English, he was a patron of the arts, notably of Edmund Spenser in his composition of The Faerie Queene (1589–96).'

The Ralegh works studied in detail by Brushfield are:

A Bibliography of Sir Walter Ralegh (1st ed.,1886; 2nd ed., 1908)

After an apology in the preface to the first edition for the length nd detail used of the works written by, or relating to, Sir Walter

Ralegh, Thomas Brushfield writes:

> ..an enlarged plan appears to possess many advantages. It
> presents a favourable opportunity of giving additional
> particulars, and of adding extended notes to the various works
> noticed, so as to make it of more practical value. By pointing
> out the dates, titles, etc., of any reprints, references are
> facilitated ; and by bringing into association a larger number of
> works under the same heading than would be advisable or
> practicable in the instance of a general work on the county,
> there results not simply a barren record of the titles of works,
> but a kind of connected literary history of the subject chosen.
> That such a plan, carried out with respect to other individuals,
> etc., would be of future service to county and other
> bibliographers, can scarcely be denied.[2]

Brushfield had an analytical approach to his work and looked
closely for comparative detail with which to reach his conclusions.
Brushfield cites examples of his method:

> It appears at first sight somewhat remarkable that so few of
> (Ralegh's) works were printed during his lifetime. The first,
> published in 1591, was *A report of the truth of the fight about
> the Isles of Agores* ; the second, in 1596, *The Discoverie of
> Guiana* ; and in 1614, the *History of the World*: this is the
> complete list. This was mainly due to the majority of his works
> having been written during the reign of James I., when many
> obstacles prevented their publication. As a substitute for this,
> however, a large number of MS copies of his writings appear

to have been circulated, and Oldys, in his Life of Sir W. Ralegh testifies to this fact ; the British Museum, Bodleian, Dr. Williams', and other libraries, possess many of these.

The majority of his minor works were not published until after the death of Charles I. Doubts have been raised as to his having been the author of several attributed to him. It is certain that his name appears on the title pages of some that were known to have been written by others. (*"Rawleigh Redivivus "* heads the title-page of the Life of the Earl of Shaftesbury published in 1683.) Of the great popularity of his works we have ample evidence in the number of editions of some of them, e.g. the *History of the World and the Remains*. The *Discoverie of Guiana* was translated into many of the European languages. With few exceptions, all the works in the accompanying list have been carefully examined. As far as was practicable, the various editions of every work have been carefully collated with each other. This was notably the case with the *History of the World and the Remains*, and also with the various articles contained in the latter.

I may draw attention to the Observations touching trade . . . with the Hollander, published under various titles, which were somewhat puzzling to unravel at first ; but a careful comparison of all the versions, made at one sitting at the British Museum Library, showed that they were all essentially one and the same work, each with variations which I have noticed under their respective titles. In all cases I have endeavoured to make the notes as practical and as useful as possible. Perhaps no celebrity has had his biography more frequently written than Sir Walter ; and though the list be long, other accounts were contemplated by Gibbon, J. Payne Collier, Macvey Napier, W. Hepworth Dixon, and Martin Tupper.

.....Foreign editions and translations are, as a rule, mentioned in the notices of the English works. With respect to the Poems and Letters, only the collected editions have been included in the list. Lists of Sir Walter Ralegh's works have appeared in the following : J. Shirley, Life of Sir W. R. (1677), 243. Wood's Ath. Oxon. (1661) ; much enlarged in edition by Bliss (1815).

In his preface to the second edition Brushfield explains the need for modifications and indicates that:

In my 80th year, and with rapidly failing eyesight, I have been unable to correct the printer's proofs, or to render any assistance in the preparation of this edition for the press. All this has, however, been most kindly undertaken by Mr. James Henry Commin, the son of my publisher. To the latter I am also greatly indebted for his counsel and active assistance in the final preparation of the work.

This is the work that, in 1908, earned Dr Thomas Brushfield his deserved reputation as greatest living Ralegh scholar.

A number of volumes appeared, the first of which was:

Raleghana Parts 1 - VIII (1896, 1898, 1900, 1902 - 7)

being a series of papers delivered by Thomas Brushfield to the

Devonshire Association. The final paper was provided to the Association's 1907 Axminster meeting. These papers were later aggregated and published as this book. The subjects covered are many and various and include most of the myths and truths surrounding Ralegh's interesting life. The discoveries of tobacco and potato feature as well as the numerous piratical ventures of Ralegh in pursuit of prize ships flying foreign flags.

The Birthplace of Sir Walter Ralegh (1889)
Dr Brushfield lived in Budleigh, just a short drive from the East Budleigh farmhouse known as Hayes Barton. It still exists in an excellent state of preservation. This is an archaeologist's examination of the building and its *environs*.

Notes on the Ralegh Family (1883)
The earliest notice of Sir Walter Ralegh known to exist was found and communicated to the Transactions of the Devonshire Association in 1883.

Sir Walter Ralegh; a Plea for a Surname (1886)
This is a reference to a deed preserved in Sidmouth Church, by which tithes of fish are leased by the manor of Sidmouth to 'Walter Rawlegh the elder, Carow Ralegh, and Walter Ralegh the younger,' on September 10, 1560. In 1578 the same persons passed over their interest in the fish-titles in another deed, which contains their signatures. It is amusing to find that the family had not decided how to spell its name. The father writes 'Ralegh,' his elder son Carew writes 'Caro Rawlyh,' while the subject of this memoir, in this his earliest known signature, calls himself 'Rauleygh.'

Sir Walter `Ralegh and his "History of the World"
(1887)

The conjecture that surrounds this work is enormous and in his book Brushfield attempts to examine the whole work in detail. Not always successfully in some later authors' opinions!

Ralegh Miscellanea Parts I and II (1909 - 10)

By now Brushfield was nearly finished with his bibliography and papers he had presented to the Devonshire Association. This is his final word on the subject.

Chapter 14

1502? - 1618

Ralegh Literary Heritage

It was doubtless by association with the sailors on the beach at Budleigh Salterton that he imbibed the almost instinctive understanding of the sea that characterises his writings. Sir John Millais, in his picture 'The Boyhood of Ralegh,' painted at Budleigh Salterton in 1870, represents him sitting on the seashore at the foot of a sunburnt sailor, who is narrating his adventures. He certainly learnt to speak with the broadest of Devonshire accents, which he retained through life. From childhood he was, says Naunton, 'an indefatigable reader.' At the age of fourteen or fifteen he would seem to have gone to Oxford, where he was, according to Wood, in residence for three years as a member of Oriel College. His name appears in the college books in 1572, but the dates and duration of his residence are uncertain.

In the spring of 1576 he was in London, and in a copy of congratulatory verses which he prefixed to the 'Steele Glas' of George Gascoigne, published in April 1576, he is described as 'of the Middle Temple.' It may be supposed that he was only 'a passing lodger;' he has himself stated that he was not a law student (Works, i. 669). In December 1577 he appears to have had a residence at Islington, and been known as a hanger-on of the court (Gosse, p. 6).

Sweet were the sauce would please each kind of

taste ;
The life likewise were pure that never swerved :
For spiteful tongues in cankered stomachs placed
Deem worst of things which best deserved.
But what for that?   This medicine may suffice
To scorn the rest, and seek to please the wise.

The friendship of Leicester, and, through Sidney, of Walsingham, brought Ralegh opportunities of personal distinction. In August he was joined in commission with Sir Warham St. Leger for the trial of James Fitzgerald, brother of the Earl of Desmond, who was sentenced and put to death as a traitor. Ralegh expressed the conviction that leniency to bloody-minded malefactors was cruelty to good and peaceable subjects.

The only fault found by the queen was that the superior officers had been spared (Cal. State Papers, Ireland, lxxix. 13). Edmund Spenser, who was present at Smerwick, approved of Grey's order and of Ralegh's obedience (View of the Present State of Ireland, Globe edit. p. 656), and Mendoza, the Spanish ambassador in London, ventured on no remonstrance (Froude, Hist. of England, Cabinet edit. x. 582–91).

During the campaign Spenser and Ralegh were necessarily brought together, but it does not appear that any intimacy then sprang up between them, and in January Ralegh was sent into garrison at Cork, where, except for an occasional journey to Dublin to confer with Grey or a dashing skirmish, he lay till the end of July.

There is nothing improbable in the story of his spreading his new plush cloak over a muddy road for the queen to walk on. The evidence on which it is based (Fuller, Worthies) is shadowy; but the incident is in keeping with Ralegh's quick, decided resolution, and it is certain that Ralegh sprang with a sudden bound into the royal favour. Fuller's other story of his writing on a window of the palace, with a diamond,

Fain would I climb, yet fear I to fall,
and of Elizabeth's replying to it with
If thy heart fails thee, climb not at all.

Fain would I

rests on equally weak testimony, and is inherently improbable.

It appears that he possessed a handsome figure and face and these were his real credentials. He was under thirty, tall, well-built, of 'a good presence,' with thick dark hair, a bright complexion, and an expression full of life. His dress, too, was at all times magnificent, to the utmost limit of his purse; and, when called on to speak, he answered 'with a bold and plausible tongue, whereby he could set out his parts to the best advantage.' He had, moreover, the reputation of a bold and dashing partisan, ingenious and daring; fearless alike in the field and in the council-chamber, a man of a stout heart and a sound head.

Ralegh was ill-fitted to spend his life in luxury and court intrigue, of which, as the queen's favourite, he was the centre.

If all the world and love were young,
And truth in every shepherd's tongue,
These pretty pleasures might me move
To live with thee, and be thy love.

The Nymph's Reply to the Passionate Shepherd.

To Ralegh belongs the credit of having, first of Englishmen, pointed out the way to the formation of a greater England beyond the seas. But he had no personal share in the actual expeditions, and he was never in his whole life near the coast of Virginia.

Among the more immediate results of his endeavours is popularly reckoned the introduction, about 1586, into England of potatoes and tobacco. The assertion is in part substantiated. His 'servant' Harriot, whom he sent out to America, gives in his 'Brief and True Report of Virginia' (1588) a detailed account of the potato and tobacco, and describes the uses to which the natives put them; he himself made the experiment of smoking tobacco. The potato and tobacco were in 1596 growing as rare plants in Lord Burghley's garden in the Strand (Gerard, Catalogus, 1596). In his 'Herbal' (1597, pp. 286–8, 781) Gerard gives an illustration and description of each. Although potatoes had at a far earlier period been brought to Europe by the Spaniards, Harriot's specimens were doubtless the earliest to be planted in this kingdom. Some of them Ralegh planted in his garden at Youghal, and on that ground he may be regarded as one of Ireland's chief benefactors. This claim is supported by the statement made to the Royal Society in 1693 by Sir Robert Southwell, then president, to the effect that his grandfather first cultivated the potato in Ireland from specimens given him by Ralegh (G. W. Johnson, Gardener, 1849, i. 8).

It is stated in every 'Life' of Ralegh that when the contending fleets were coming up Channel, Ralegh was one of the volunteers who joined the lord admiral and took a more or less prominent part in the subsequent fighting. Of this there is no mention in the English state papers or in the authentic correspondence of the time. Nor can any reliance be placed on the report that Ralegh took part in the naval operations mentioned in the 'Copie of a Letter sent out of England to Don Bernardin Mendoza' (1588, and often reprinted) (cf. A Pack of Spanish Lies). This doubtful authority also credits Robert Cecil with having joined the fleet—a manifest misstatement (Defeat of the Spanish Armada, i. 342).

To this period may be referred his intimacy with Edmund Spenser [q. v.], who bestowed on him in his poems the picturesque appellation of 'The Shepherd of the Ocean.' Ralegh returned to court in October, and, taking Spenser with him, secured for the poet a warm welcome from the queen.

He was staying at his own residence, Durham House in the Strand, the ancient London house of the bishops of Durham, which he held since 1584 on a grant from the crown then in July he was sent to the Tower.

His recall and imprisonment were due to the queen's wrath on discovering that the man whom she had delighted to honour and enrich, who had been professing a lover's devotion to her, had been carrying on an intrigue with one of her maids of honour, Elizabeth, daughter of Sir Nicholas Throgmorton [q. v.], who, baptised at Beddington 16 April 1565, was 27 years old. In March it was rumoured that Ralegh had married the lady, but this, in a letter to Robert Cecil on 10 March 1592, Ralegh had denounced as a 'malicious report.' According to Camden, Ralegh seduced the lady some months before, an assertion which J. P. Collier needlessly attempted to corroborate by printing a forged news-letter on the topic (Archæologia, xxxiv. 160–70).

The queen showed no more mercy to Mistress Throgmorton than to her lover, and she also was imprisoned in the Tower. In a letter

addressed to Sir Robert Cecil in July Ralegh affected frenzied grief
and rage at being debarred from the presence of the queen, whose
personal attractions he eulogised in language of absurd extravagance
(Edwards, ii. 51–2). In his familiar poem

> As you came from the holy land
>   Of Walsinghame,
> Met you not with my true love
>   By the way as you came ?
>
> How shall I know your true love,
>   That have met many one,
> As I went to the holy land,
>   That have come, that have gone ?
>
> She is neither white nor brown,
>   But as the heavens fair ;
> There is none hath a form so divine
>   In the earth or the air.
>
> Such a one did I meet, good sir,
>   Such an angel-like face,
> Who like a queen, like a nymph, did appear,
>   By her gait, by her grace.
>
> She hath left me here all alone,
>   All alone, as unknown,
> Who sometimes did me lead with herself,
>   And me loved as her own.

What's the cause that she leaves you alone,
   And a new way doth take,
Who loved you once as her own,
   And her joy did you make ?

I have loved her all my youth,
   But now old, as you see,
Love likes not the falling fruit
   From the withered tree.

Know that Love is a careless child,
   And forgets promise past ;
He is blind, he is deaf when he list,
   And in faith never fast.

His desire is a dureless content,
   And a trustless joy ;
He is won with a world of despair,
   And is lost with a toy.

Of womankind such indeed is the love,
   Or the word love abusèd,
Under which many childish desires
   And conceits are excusèd.

But true love is a durable fire,
   In the mind ever burning,
Never sick, never old, never dead,

From itself never turning.

In 'As you came from the Holy Land,' Ralegh seems to have converted into verse much of the flattering description of Elizabeth which figured in this letter to Cecil (Poems, ed. Hannah, pp. 80–1). But, despite these blandishments, he continued a close prisoner till the middle of September, when, on the arrival of the great carrack, the Madre de Dios, at Dartmouth, he was sent thither with Cecil and Drake, in the hope that by his local influence he might be able to stop the irregular pillage of the prize. He arrived in charge of a Mr. Blunt (State Papers, Dom. ccxliii. 17), perhaps Sir Christopher Blount [q. v.], the stepfather and friend of the Earl of Essex.

It is probable that Ralegh and Elizabeth Throgmorton were married immediately afterwards. Being forbidden to come to court, they settled at Sherborne, where in January 1591–2 Ralegh had obtained a ninety-nine years' lease of the castle and park.

Passionately devoted to literature and science, he associated in London with men of letters of all classes and tastes. He was, with Cotton and Selden, a member of the Society of Antiquaries that had been formed by Archbishop Parker and lasted till 1605 (Archæologia, I. XXV), and to him is assigned the first suggestion of those meetings at the Mermaid tavern in Bread Street which Shakespeare, Ben Jonson, and many lesser writers long graced with their presence.

He made valuable suggestions to Richard Hakluyt, when he was designing his great collection of 'Voyages' (cf. History of the World, bk. ii. cap. iii. sect. viii.). But it was not only literary and archæological topics that Ralegh discussed with his literary or antiquarian friends. Although he did not personally adopt the scepticism in matters of religion which was avowed by many Elizabethan authors, it attracted his speculative cast of mind, and he sought among the sceptics his closest companions. Thomas Harriot, who acknowledged himself to be a deist, he took into his house, on his return from Virginia, in order to study mathematics with him. With Christopher Marlowe, whose religious views were equally heterodox, he was in equally confidential relations. Izaak Walton testifies that he wrote the well-known answer to Marlowe's familiar lyric, 'Come, live with me and be my love.'

> Come live with me and be my love,
> And we will all the pleasures prove
> That valleys, groves, hills, and fields,
> Woods or steepy mountain yields.
>
> And we will sit upon the rocks,
> Seeing the shepherds feed their flocks,
> By shallow rivers to whose falls
> Melodious birds sing madrigals.

There is little doubt that Ralegh, Harriot, and Marlowe, and some other personal friends, including Ralegh's brother Carew, were all in 1592 and 1593 members of a select coterie which frequently debated religious topics with perilous freedom. According to a catholic pamphleteer writing in 1592, and calling himself Philopatris, the society was known as 'Sir Walter Rawley's School of Atheisme.' The master was stated to be a conjuror (doubtless a reference to Harriot), and 'much diligence was said to be used to get young gentlemen to this school, wherein both Moyses and our Sauior, the old and the new Testaments are iested at and the schollers taught among other things to spell God backwards' (An Advertisement written to a Secretarie of my L. Treasurers of Ingland by an Inglishe Intelligencer, 1592, p. 18).

In May 1593 the coterie's proceedings were brought to the notice of the privy council. A warrant was issued for the arrest of Marlowe and another, but Marlowe died next month, before it took effect. Ralegh had doubtless returned to Sherborne after the dissolution of parliament on 10 April. But later in the year the lord keeper, Puckering, made searching inquiries into Ralegh's and his friends' relations with the freethinking dramatist. A witness deposed that Marlowe had read an atheistical lecture to Ralegh and others.

On 21 March 1593–4 a special commission, headed by Thomas Howard, viscount Bindon, was directed to pursue the investigation at Cerne in Dorset, in the neighbourhood of Sherborne, and to examine Ralegh, his brother Carew, 'Mr. Thynne of Wiltshire,' and 'one Heryott of Sir Walter Rawleigh's house' as to their alleged heresies. Unfortunately the result of the investigation is not accessible (Harl. MS. 7042, p. 401) [see Kyd, Thomas; Marlowe, Christopher]. In June 1594 Ralegh spent a whole night in eagerly discussing religious topics with the Jesuit John Cornelius [q. v.], while the latter lay under arrest at Wolverton (Foley, Jesuits, iii. 461–2).

Ralegh's accuracy as a topographer and cartographer of Guiana or the central district of Venezuela has been established by subsequent explorers, nor is there reason to doubt that the gold-mine which he sought really existed.

For the next few weeks he seems to have been on familiar, almost friendly, terms with Essex. Meantime the intelligence from Spain showed that Philip was preparing to take revenge for the loss he had sustained at Cadiz. Ralegh drew up a paper entitled 'Opinion on the Spanish Alarum,' in support of the contention that the cheapest and surest way to defend England was to strike beforehand at Spain. The idea had been forcibly urged by Drake ten years before, but the time was now more favourable and the advice accorded with the queen's inclinations. During the years immediately following, his time was, for the most part, divided between the court and the west country, with an occasional visit to Ireland. In 1597 he was chosen member of parliament for Dorset, and in 1601 for Cornwall. In the last parliament he defended monopolies, which were attacked with much heat in a debate of 19 Nov. 1601.

He is reported to have blushed when a fellow-member spoke of the iniquity of a monopoly of playing-cards, and he elaborately explained his relations with the monopoly of tin, which he owned as lord warden of the stannaries, but he said nothing of his equally valuable monopoly of sweet wines (D'Ewes, Journals of Parliaments, p. 645).

But the old quarrel with Essex was still smouldering. In season and out of season, Essex and his partisans, especially Sir Christopher Blount [q. v.], were loud in their denunciations of Ralegh. Essex, writing to the queen on 25 June 1599, accused him of 'wishing the ill-success of your majesty's most important action, the decay of your greatest strength, and the destruction of your faithfullest servants' (Edwards, i. 254), and at the last he asserted that it was to counteract Ralegh's plots that he had come over from Ireland, and 'pretended that he took arms principally to save himself from Cobham and Ralegh, who, he gave out, should have murdered him in his house'

(Cecil to Sir George Carew).

Ralegh was not disposed to submit meekly to this active hostility. At an uncertain date—probably in 1601—he wrote of Essex to Cecil: 'If you take it for a good counsel to relent towards this tyrant, you will repent it when it shall be too late. His malice is fixed, and will not evaporate by any your mild courses. ... For after revenges, fear them not; for your own father was esteemed to be the contriver of Norfolk's ruin, yet his son followeth your father's son and loveth him' (cf. St. John, ii. 38; and Devereux, Lives of the Devereux, ii. 177).

> O eloquent, just, and mightie Death! whom none could advise, thou hast perswaded; what none hath dared, thou hast done; and whom all the world hath flattered, thou only hast cast out of the world and despised. Thou hast drawne together all the farre stretchèd greatnesse, all the pride, crueltie, and ambition of man, and covered it all over with these two narrow words, Hic jacet!
>
> Historie of the World. Book v. Part 1.

When Essex was brought out for execution, Ralegh was present, but withdrew on hearing it murmured that he was there to feast his eyes on his enemy's sufferings. Blount afterwards admitted that neither he nor Essex had really believed that Ralegh had plotted against the earl's life; 'it was,' he said, 'a word cast out to colour other matters;' and on the scaffold he entreated pardon of Ralegh, who was again present, possibly in his official capacity as captain of the guard. His attitude towards Essex and his party seems to have led Sir Amyas Preston to send him, in 1602, a challenge, which he accepted.

He arranged his papers and affairs as a precautionary measure, entailing the Sherborne estate on his son Walter; but for some unexplained reason the duel did not take place.

Ralegh fell into disfavour and was brought to trial. Two days before Ralegh's trial, Watson, George Brooke, and four others were tried and condemned; a week later, Cobham and Grey. Ralegh was ordered to be executed on 11 Dec., and, in full expectation of death, he wrote a touching letter of farewell to his wife.

Dear Wife,

Thou shall receive my last words in these my last lines; my love I send you that you may keepe it when I am dead, and my counsel that you may remember it when I am no more. I would not with my will present you sorrows (dear Besse) let them go to the grave with me, and be buried in the dust. And seeing it is not the will of God that ever I shall see you any more in this life, beare my destruction gently, and with a heart like your selfe.

First, I send you all the thanks which my heart can conceive, or my words expresse, for your many troubles and cares taken for me, which though they have not taken effect as you wished, yet my debt to you is not lesse, but I shall never recompence it in this world.

Secondly, I beseech you even for the love you bare me living, that you do not hide your selfe many dayes, but by your travell seek to helpe your miserable fortune, and the right of your poore childe: Your mourning cannot availe me that I am but dust.

Thirdly, you shall understand that my Lands were conveied (bona fide) to my childe, the writings were drawne at Mid summer twelve-month, as divers can witnesse, and I trust that my blood will quench their malice that desire my slaughter, and that they will not seek also to kill you and yours with extream poverty.

To what friend to direct you I know not, for all mine have left me in the true time of tyall; most sorry I am (as God knoweth) that being thus surprised with death I can leave you no better estate; I meant you all my Office of wines or that I should purchase by selling it, halfe my stuffe and my jewels, (but some for the boy) but God hath prevented all my determinations; The great God that worketh in all.

But if you can live free from want, care for no more, for the rest is but vanity.

This was published in 1644 with a few other small pieces in a volume entitled 'To-day a Man, To-morrow None,' in the 'Arraignment' of 1648, and in the 'Remaines' of 1651 (cf. Edwards, ii. 284). But on 10 Dec. Ralegh, with Cobham and Grey, was reprieved; on the 16th the three were sent up to London and committed to the Tower. All Ralegh's offices were vacated by his attainder, and his estates forfeited, but his personal property was now restored to him. In 1602, when he had assigned the manor of Sherborne to trustees for the benefit of his son Walter, he reserved the income from it to himself for life.

Ralegh was treated leniently in prison. He had apartments in the upper story of the Bloody Tower, where his wife and son, with their personal attendants, also lived, at the rate, for household expenses, of about 200l. a year. But his health suffered from cold (Notes and Queries, 2nd ser. viii. 107), and frequent efforts were made by his enemies to concoct fresh charges of disloyalty against him. In 1610 they succeeded in depriving him for three months of the society of his wife, who was ordered to leave the Tower. In Prince Henry, however, he found a useful friend. The prince was mainly attracted by Ralegh's studies in science and literature, to which his enforced leisure was devoted. For the prince, Ralegh designed a model of a ship. Encouraged by him, he began his 'History of the World,' and for his guidance designed many political treatises. In a laboratory, or 'still-house,' allowed him in the Tower garden for chemical and philosophical experiments, he condensed fresh from salt water (an art only practised generally during the nineteenth century) (cf. Cal. State Papers, Dom. 1606–7), and compounded drugs, chief among which was his 'Great Cordial or Elixir.' Ralegh's own prescription is not extant, but Nicholas le Febre compounded it in the presence of Charles II on 20 Sept. 1662 (Evelyn, Diary, ii. 152), and printed an account of the demonstration in 1664. At the same time whatever books Ralegh chose to buy or borrow were freely at his disposal, and he interested himself in the scientific researches of his fellow-prisoner, Henry Percy, ninth earl of Northumberland, into whose service he introduced Harriot, his old friend and fellow-worker.

He had nothing to do but throw himself on the king's mercy; whereupon the chief justice, Sir Henry Montagu (afterwards Earl of Manchester), awarded execution according to law.

On the following morning, 29 Oct., he was brought to the scaffold erected in Old Palace Yard. He met his death calmly and cheerfully, and of his last words many have become almost proverbial. As he laid his head on the block some one objected that it ought to be towards the east. 'What matter,' he answered, 'how the head lie, so the heart be right?' than which, says Mr. Gardiner, no better epitaph could be found for him. An official 'Declaration' of his demeanour and carriage was issued a few days later and was frequently reprinted. His remains were delivered to his wife, and they were buried in the chancel of St. Margaret's Church, Westminster, in spite of Lady Ralegh's wish that he should be buried at Beddington; the head she caused to be embalmed, and she kept it by her in a red leather bag as long as she lived. It seems to have passed into the possession of her son Carew, but what ultimately became of it is uncertain. A memorial window was placed in 1882 by American citizens in St. Margaret's Church, with an inscription by James Russell Lowell.

> Go, Soul, the body's guest,
> Upon a thankless arrant:
> Fear not to touch the best,
> The truth shall be thy warrant:
> Go, since I needs must die,
> And give the world the lie.
>
> The Lie.

The chief Lives of Ralegh are those by William Oldys, first published in 1736 (here referred to in the 8vo edition of 1829), by Thomas Birch, (1751), by Arthur Cayley (1805), by Patrick Fraser-Tytler (1833), by Edward Edwards (2 vols. 1868), by J. A. St. John (1868), and by Mr. William Stebbing (1891). Gibbon contemplated a Life of Ralegh, but abandoned the notion on reading that by Oldys. The Life by Edwards, which embodies numerous original letters and documents, is a rich quarry of material, but scarcely a connected or accurate narrative. Although no detailed references are given to original authorities by Mr. Stebbing, his biography is of all the most readable and best informed. That by Mr. Edmund Gosse (1886) is, like sketches by Macvey Napier and Charles Kingsley, an entertaining essay. For the history of Ralegh's parents and his early life, see pedigree in Howard's Miscellanea Genealogica et Heraldica, ii. 155–7; and the invaluable papers by Dr. Brushfield of Budleigh Salterton in the Transactions of the Devonshire Association. But a good many points in Ralegh's Elizabethan career remain obscure. The most authentic sources for it are the State Papers, Domestic and Ireland; the Calendars both of the Carew MSS. and of the Cecil Papers.

The Privy Council Register throws little light on Ralegh's curious relations with Marlowe in 1592–3, which are here noticed for the first time. Sir John Pope-Hennessy's Sir Walter Ralegh in Ireland (1883); Sir Walter Ralegh and his Colony in America, by the Rev. Increase N. Tarbox, Boston (Prince Society), 1884, which reprints Harriot's Report, and Sir Robert Hermann Schomburgk's introduction to his edition of the Discoverie of Guiana (1848) are all useful.

A complete account of Ralegh's public life from the accession of James I is given in the History of England by Mr. S. R. Gardiner, who, while utilising the labours of his predecessors, has corrected or illustrated them by his own researches among original documents both in England and in Spain. See also Wood's Athenæ Oxon. ed. Bliss, ii. 235–9; John Ford's Linea Vitæ, 1620; Naunton's Fragmenta Regalia, 1641; Fuller's Worthies (1662); Lloyd's Worthies (1665); Notes and Queries, 8th ser. x. 211; Aubrey's Lives, and Spedding's Life of Bacon. For Ralegh's literary work the chief authorities are the introduction to Dr. Hannah's edition of his Poems (1885), Dr. Brushfield's Bibliography of Ralegh (Plymouth, 1886, new ed. Exeter, 1908), his Bibliography of the History of the World (1886), and his Sir Walter Ralegh and his History of the World (1887). [3]

Chapter 15

1850 - 1910

Memberships

Dr Thomas Nadauld Brushfield was a member of the Devonshire Association from 1882 - 1910 and was president in 1893 when he delivered the presidential address on the Literature of Devonshire before the year 1640. Hardly a year passed without a paper being delivered to meetings of the Association. After his death in 1910 both his wife and Dr Archibald Brushfield also joined the Association.

The Association published the following obituary notice:

By the death of Dr. Brushfield the Association suffers an irreparable loss. One of its most active and prominent members, he was a regular contributor to its Transactions, and a constant attendant at its Annual Meetings, where his genial presence and good-humour will be greatly missed.
Dr. Brushfield belonged to an old Derbyshire family.

He died on 28th November, 1910, in his 82nd year and is buried in Budleigh Salterton.

He was a Fellow of the Society of Antiquaries and a local secretary of that body and contributed a number of papers to the meetings.

The Society of Antiquaries of London is charged by its Royal Charter of 1751 with 'the encouragement, advancement and furtherance of the study and knowledge of the antiquities and history of this and other countries'. It celebrated its Tercentenary in 2007.The Society's 2,900 Fellows include many distinguished archaeologists and art and architectural historians holding positions of responsibility across the cultural heritage. The Fellowship is international in its reach and its interests are inclusive of all aspects of the material past.

Brushfield was ex-President of the Devonshire Branch of the British Medical Association and, before this, was a member of the Chester Medical Society; the Medico-Psychological Association. Though he published papers dealing with the development of treatments for the insane most of his books and papers were published after he retired to Devon and, though some of his papers were delivered to meetings of the medical associations most of his work dealt with his favoured subject of bibliography.

He was also founder of the Devon and Cornwall Record Society and his other memberships include: the Chester Archaeological Society; the Derbyshire Archaeological Society, the Teign Naturalists' Field Club; the Torquay Natural History Society.

He was a church warden at All Saints, East Budleigh where he wrote and published his researches into this parish and those surrounding.

Thomas Brushfield was a leading member of the committee entrusted with the building of St. Peter's Church in Budleigh Salterton and is widely credited with bringing about the foundation of this church, firstly as a chapel-at-ease and later, in 1900, its foundation as the parish church in Budleigh Salterton.

Unsurprisingly, he was greatly interested in local affairs and was at one time both a member of the Local Board and of its successor the Urban District Council.

Together with Dr Foster he took a leading part in the building and organization of the Cottage Hospital of which he was vice-president and one of the trustees for ten years.

He was a director of the Budleigh Salterton Railway Company from its inception to the day of his death and was credited with bringing the railway to Budleigh both as a branch of the Sidmouth line and its extension to Exmouth.

For twenty five years he was secretary or chairman of the Budleigh Salterton Croquet Club where he established the lawn tennis section and was its President in 1895.

Mostly to provide fund raising events for the hospital and croquet club he promoted and acted in concerts and amateur theatricals.

He died on 28th November, 1910, in his 82nd year and is buried in St Peter's churchyard in Budleigh Salterton.

Writing in the January 21st edition of the Western Weekly News under the headline "Western Representative Men" W.H.K Wright said:

It will be seen that in the quiet retirement of Budleigh Salterton the subject of our sketch has led a very active life; and that he has done much valuable work to the memory of one of the greatest, if not the greatest Devonians. His geniality and humour endear him to everyone with whom he is brought into contact; he is a very happy and entertaining speaker, his speeches being generally bright and sparkling with wit; but it is in the smaller and more select circle of his friends and intimates that he is perhaps best appreciated.

In the Dictionary of National Biography extracts from his entry read:

Lunacy specialist and antiquary, born in London on 10 December 1828, was son of Thomas Brushfield, of an ancient Derbyshire family, J.P. and D.L. of the Tower of London, by his wife Susannah Shepley. His grandfather, George Brushfield married Ann Nadauld, great granddaughter of Henri Nadauld, a Huguenot who, settling in England after the revocation of the Edict of Nantes, became a sculptor and in 1698 decorated Chatsworth House with statuary and friezes....

.... Brushfield was a pioneer of 'non restraint' treatment of lunatics. He sought to lighten the patents' life in asylums by making the wards cheerful and by organising entertainments. His contribution to the literature of lunacy includes 'Medical Certificates of Insanity' (Lancet, 1880) and Practical Hints on the 'Symptoms, Treatment and Medico-Legal Aspects of Insanity' which was read before the Chester Medical Society in 1890.

On his retirement from professional work in 1882 Dr Brushfield settled at Budleigh Salterton, on the East Devon Coast, near Hayes Barton, the birthplace of Sir Walter Ralegh. Brushfield made the career of Ralegh his main study for the rest of his life. He became a member of the Devonshire Association in 1882, was elected to he council in 1863, and was president in 1893-4. A paper, 'Notes on the Ralegh Family' which he read before the 1883 meeting of the Association (Trans. xv. 1883) proved the first of a long series of papers called 'Raleghana,' embodying minutest research into Ralegh's life and literary work, which were published in the same 'Transactions' between 1896 and 1907. 'Ralegh Miscellanea' (pts i. And ii.) followed in 1909 – 10. He contributed many other papers on the same and cognate themes to other archaeological journals. He was a reader for the 'New English Dictionary,' and contributed over 72,000 slips (see preface, vol. I.). His bibliography of Ralegh which was published in book form in 1896 (2nd edt. 1908 with photographic portrait), first appeared serially in the 'Western Antiquary,' vol 5, 1885 – 6.

Brushfield was a freemason, was elected F.S.A. in 1899 and was a founder of the Devon and Cornwall Record Society. He was a popular lecturer in the west country and his lantern slides are now in the Exeter Public Library, together with the more important Ralegh items from his library. The rest of his library of about 10,000 volumes and manuscripts, many of local interest, was dispersed after is death. He died at Budleigh Salterton on 28 November 1910, and was buried there. He married on 5 Aug. 1852, Hannah, daughter of John Davis of London, who survived him with three sons and three daughters.

Epilogue

It is now over 100 years since Thomas Brushfield died from a chill caught following his visit to the annual meeting of the Chester Archaeology Society, when aged 82 years, almost to the day. Hannah went on living in the town in Marine Parade, close by the sea wall where Millais painted his famous picture, until her death in 1919. Both of them would easily recognise the Budleigh Salterton of today.

There have been changes since Edwardian times but the sea front, beach and red sandstone cliffs remain the same and the High Street has a very similar collection of shops. Fewer butchers grocers, fruit and vegetable purveyors, perhaps, but the buildings remain much as they were.

Cricket stopped in 1914 and did not recommence until 1922 when a new ground was positioned somewhat optimistically on the Otter Valley flood plain. Despite all vicissitudes the club remains in good heart. Many county cricketers have cut their teeth on the ground, including the well known Somerset captain Ben Brocklehurst. After the Great War, the football club, so well supported by Thomas Brushfield, still thrives.

Dr Brushfield would have been very surprised, though pleased, at the success of the East Devon Golf Club which came to Budleigh as a result of an investment by Lord Clinton who leased the fields to the club in 1902. Starting as an 9 hole though later an 18 hole course it has been progressively eroded by cliff falls as the sea has attempted to win back its own. Had this happened in his time Thomas Brushfield would probably have been one of the first committee members!

After golf, the croquet club is the fastest growing sport following the full development of its three acre site at the top of the hill overlooking the town. This is quite probably a result of the excellent start it received during General Goodwyn's and Dr Brushfield's time. It is now one of the best in equipped in Britain with a strong membership, 10 excellent lawns and a bowling green. The *Caretaker of the Grounds* is now Chris Root though he is no longer expected to cut the lawns using a horse mower before breakfast. During the summer at least six and up to ten international tournaments are held, attracting visitors from all over the world.

Brushfield might be surprised to see the 1920's town hall, an iconic design by by Col. Hatchard Smith, war hero and London architect who came to live in the town in 1928. Responsible for building many easily-recognised large houses in Budleigh, Hachard Smith used his London practice to recommend the delights of East Devon to those of his clients wishing to enjoy a soft climate and interesting social life.

The story is told about Watch Hill, the imposing house built in 1928 above the town; an American judge approached the Hatchard Smith practice looking for a seaside place in which to live. The site was procured and building started. Just before completion Hatchard Smith had fallen for the judge's daughter and for a wedding gift he received Watch Hill and lived there until after his 100th birthday. He opened his house to Commonwealth visitors during the 1939 - 45 war. Many prominent people signed the visitors's book.

Dr Brushfield's house, The Cliff, still stands overlooking the sea though it is now split into two apartments. His beloved garden is now built over.

The churches of All Saints in East Budleigh and St Peter's in Salterton, so well served by Thomas Brushfield for 28 years, continue to thrive though there is still no prospect of adding the tower and spire to St Peter's as originally designed by architect Fellowes-Prynne. The reason then given was the need to deflect the balance of funds designated for the purpose to found a church in the village of Knowle just north of Budleigh. Times change and this small church finally closed its doors in 2013 when the site was sold. Both remaining churches with that of Otterton are now joined in a *Mission* under the direction of the Rev'd Anne Charlton.

The Cottage hospital has survived many NHS reorganisations since Miss Lewis' day but continues to exist for no better reason than that it is well supported and immensely valued by residents not only of Budleigh but of nearby Exmouth as well.

The railways into Exmouth and Sidmouth Juction and thence on to London and other parts have not fared well as a result of the Beeching Report and were closed in 1967. Brushfield, who worked so hard to establish the railways would have shared the public's general disappointment at such closures.

Brushfield did not live to see the foundation of the delightful Fairlynch Museum and its internationally-important historic costume collection. Founded as a result of the prescience of Priscilla Hull and Joy Gawne, it attracts visitors from far and wide to see its collections housed in an ancient and historic thatched house in the High Street. How Dr Brushfield would approve of this.

The Oxford English Dictionary was eventually published but not during the lifetime of either Sir James Murray or Dr Brushfield whose magnificent contribution of 72,000 slips will not again be equalled.

The East End of London of today would not be recognised by Brushfield. Gone are the black areas illustrated by Booth in his poverty maps of 1899. Mostly gone are the mean dwellings and stews so well and bitterly described by Charles Dickens.

The famous Hawksmoor Christ Church in Spitalfields continues to flourish, though the makeup of the congregation has changed beyond recognition. The Huguenot immigrants have now been assimulated into the community and have spread countrywide. They have been replaced by a different set of immigrant groups and, though there is some poverty despite the efforts of the welfare state, it would not be readily recognised as such by Thomas Brushfield JP, oil and colour merchant. The orphanges and workhouses have gone, though the Barnado Homes survive and such artists as Tracey Emin and Gilbert and George have injected new life into the artistic community.

'The London' has developed into one of the world's greatest teaching hospitals and has expanded to serve a much wider population than in Thomas' day. Bethlem and Bedlam are names still in use though they have changed completely from Brushfield's time when conditions for patients were nothing short of scandalous.

The biggest change is in the modern treatment of the mentally ill. Dr Thomas Brushfield's asylums, though not those he ran, were basically prisons for the insane, not offering treatment, but incarceration and restraint. Patients who were violent to themselaves or others, or destroyed property were caged, shackled or put into strait waistcoats. New ideas were introduced in the mid 19th century that revolutionised the treatment of the mentally ill meaning that restraints were viewed as cruel and unnecessary and conditions for the patients began to improve. This was in no small part due to the ideas and efforts of Thomas Brushfield. It is sure that had he not suffered injuries inflicted in a vicious attack he would have been an even greater innovator in the implementation of such ideas.

When his fine library was dispersed in 1911 after his death many of the best volumes went to the great libraries of the world.

What of his studies of the literary works of Sir Walter Ralegh? Brushfield is still a name revered and quoted in modern evaluations of Ralegh's writings. Brushfield's published works, if not in print, are still available in specialist bookstores. There is always room for another biography of Ralegh and new and interesting directions of research still continue today.

One example that Brushfield would have loved is this by a modern researcher into the small but rich field of Raleghana:

Sir Walter Ralegh is also known to have written a sonnet entitled *Fortune Hath Taken Thee Away, My Love.* It is now

believed that Ralegh wrote this sonnet as a response to the rise
of Robert Devereux, Earl of Essex, and thus making a
complaint over his own fall from influence.

In the publication of the sonnet Gordon Braden has
reiterated the belief amongst scholars that 'Fortune' was a code
name for the Earl of Essex and that Ralegh was informing
Elizabeth that this brought him 'to woe' and that the Earl was
now 'my mortal foe'.

Fortune Hath Taken Thee Away, My Love
by Sir Walter Raleigh

Fortune hath taken thee away, my love,
My life's soul and my soul's heaven above;
Fortune hath taken thee away, my princess;
My only light and my true fancy's mistress.

Fortune hath taken all away from me,
Fortune hath taken all by taking thee.
Dead to all joy, I only live to woe,
So fortune now becomes my mortal foe.

In vain you eyes, you eyes do waste your tears,
In vain you sighs do smoke forth my despairs,
In vain you search the earth and heaven above,
In vain you search, for fortune rules in love.

Thus now I leave my love in fortune's hands,
Thus now I leave my love in fortune's bands,
And only love the sorrows due to me;
Sorrow henceforth it shall my princess be.

I joy in this, that fortune conquers kings;
Fortune that rules on earth and earthly things
Hath taken my love in spite of Cupid's might;
So blind a dame did never Cupid right.

With wisdom's eyes had but blind Cupid seen,
Then had my love my love for ever been;
But love farewell; though fortune conquer thee,
No fortune base shall ever alter me.

Gordon Braden, Sixteenth-century poetry: an annotated anthology [2005], p. 337.

A second sonnet, often argued as having been written by Elizabeth herself, mocks Raleigh in reply. For more on this the Hobbinol's blog – *Writing the English Renaissance: Elizabethan Courtly Love.*

Dr Katherine Butler has discussed this topic in more detail on one of the History SPOT podcasts entitled: *Recreational Music-Making and the Fashioning of Political or Diplomatic Relationships at the Court of Elizabeth I.* In this paper Butler argues that musical performances in the form of lute or virginal productions carried out in private chambers or in the form of more public displays shaped courtly identity and influence and acted as a carefully staged enactment to express grievances, intent, and personality at court. Butler gives various examples ranging from Lord Darley, Walter Ralegh, and Robert Devereux, 2nd Earl of Essex.

These and many other lines of enquiry serve to emphasise the importance of Brushfield's Raleghana and literary research to this present day.

Many of the papers written by Dr Brushfield from 1882 to 1908 were read to meetings of the Devonshire Association. The DA is in 2013 celebrating its 150th anniversary under the patronage of the Earl and Countess of Devon. As in Brushfield's day it is still a hub of historical, scientific, artistic and literary enquiry. Supreme among its achievements are the annual volumes of its Transactions, which contain well over 2,000 papers and countless reports from the Sections. The entire series covers an immense range of scholarly research relating to Devon and represents the greatest single repository of information about the county. It is recognized as a valuable resource throughout the world.

Finally, it is now time to take our leave of Dr Thomas Nadauld Brushfield with these words by Ralegh:

"Farewell, false love, the oracle of lies,
A mortal foe and enemy to rest;
An envious boy, from whom all cares arise,
A bastard vile, a beast with rage possessed;
A way of error, a temple full of treason,
In all effects contrary unto reason."

A Farewell to False Love (l. 1-6). Oxford Book of Sixteenth Century Verse, The. E. K. Chambers, comp. (1932) Oxford University Press.

References

Chapter 1 Beginnings (also see notes to Appendices I, II & III)

1   Weather records 1828

2   Weddings England & Wales

3   Oil and colourman Nottingham

4   David Perdue *Charles Dickens*

5   1841 census

6   Perry Wood and Louisa Berry 1830 Lambeth

7   Madison Jefferson County Public Library's History Rescue pages for the Christ Episcopal Church

Chapter 2   Nadauld Heritage

1   Brushfield family records

2   Santonge region is a small region on the Atlantic Coast now Charete-Maritime in the adminstrative region of Poitou-Charentes

The Huguenots were members of the Protestant Reformed Church of France during the 16th and 17th centuries. French Protestants were inspired by the writings of John Calvin in the 1530s, and they were called Huguenots by the 1560s. 5. IR (Inf. Stuart Band, Christopher Ridgway)

3   Hugeunot society proceedings

4   Household accounts of the Duke of Bedford and the Biography of Sculptors in Britain

5   Literary References: Thompson 1949, passim; Murdoch

References

1988, 240-1

Archival References: Poor Rates, F 1232 (1697); Castle Howard Building Accts, G2/2/27, 22 Oct 1706; G2/2/28, 22 Oct 1706; G2/2/31-34, nd; Chatsworth Building Accts vol vi, fol 1 (April 28-Aug 28, 1700); fol 16, Dec 1700-April 1701; fol 17, Feb 1701; fol 91 (1703); vol vii, fol 57 (1702); fol 63 (1703); fol 82 (1704); fol 93 (1706); vol C/21, fol 27 (1710-11); fol 40 (1713); fol 41 (1714)

6   Proceedings of the Huguenot Society

7   ibid

8   Nicholas Hawksmoor was born in Nottinghamshire in 1661, George Vertue, wrote in 1731 that he was taken as a youth to act as clerk by 'Justice Mellust in Yorkshire, where Mr Gouge senior did some fretwork ceilings afterwards Mr. Haukesmore [sic] came to London, became clerk to Sr. Christopher Wren & thence became an Architect'

9   Proceeding of the Hugeunot Society

10   Wirksworth Parish Records 1600-1900

11   "Trial of The Reverend Robert Taylor, A.B.M.R.C.S. Upon a Charge of Blasphemy, with his Defence, as Delivered by himself, Before The Lord Chief Justice and a Special Jury, on Wednesday, October 24, 1827"

12   *The Worst Street in London* Fiona Rule

13   The Jack the Ripper A-Z; Paul Begg, Martin Fido, Keith Skinner

Chapter 2   The Nadauld Heritage

1   http://philosopedia.org/index.php/Robert_Taylor. Gordon Stein

2   http://ia700506.us.archive.org

References

Chapter 3   London School University and Hospital

1   1841 and 1851 census returns

2   www.bartsandthelondon.nhs

3   Bringing Back in Victorian England: Pauper Lunatics, 1840-1870' in Bynum, Porter & Shepherd. (eds.)

4   1728 by Daniel Defoe. ... about unjust declarations of insanity, about strange views on mental illness

5   www.oldbaileyonline.org

6   Thomas Bewley Madness to Mental Illness. A history f the Royal College of Psychiatrists. Online archive 5

Chapter 4   Christ Church, Spitalfields

1   Nadauld family records

2   Birmingham Univeristy letters to Cann Hughes

Ladd 509/1 Ladd 509/2 Ladd 509/45

add 509/49 Ladd 509/50 Ladd 509/56

3   Old Bailey Court records. Deism is the belief that reason and observation of the natural world are sufficient to determine the existence of God

4   http://www.ccspitalfields.org

5   http://www.thedispensarylondon.co.uk

6   Poor Law Commissioners' Fourth Annual Report in 1838

Chapter 5   Chester County Asylum

1   *Seeing the Insane* Sander L Gilman

2   Proceedingns of the Chester Medical Society

3   Proceedings of the Chester Archaeological Society

References

Chapter 6   Wider Horizons
1   Subscriber to Vestiges of Antiquaries of Derbyshire and the Sepulchral Usages of its Inhabitants (Bateman 1848a).
2   Devon Record Office:Z19/15/5a-j

Commonplace books of T N Brushfield (10 volumes in box file)

Z19/17/3a-d Lectures and notes on obsolete punishments by T N Brushfield (4 vols)

Z19/36/14

Chapter 7   Brookwood Asylum, Woking
1   http://www.sackettfamily.info
2   OED OED catalogue

B/3/6/2 Volume of James Murray's correspondence pasted into an exercise book, including at least one letter by TB, c.1880-89.

B/4/4/2   Letter to James Murray from TB re. quotations from Leslie Stephen's 'Playground of Europe', 1895.

B/4/4/18

3. ibid

Chapter 8   Bibliophile
1   OED history extracts
2   OED catalogue

B/3/6/2 Volume of James Murray's correspondence pasted into an exercise book., c.1880-89.

B/4/4/2 Letter to James Murray from TB re. quotations from Leslie Stephen's 'Playground of Europe', 1895.

References

B/4/4/18 Lists of books lent to the OED by various individuals. TB lent: Glossographia Anglicana Nova (1719) and English Expositor by Bullokar (1616).

Chapter 9   Budleigh Salterton
1   Minutes of the Budleigh Salterton Croquet Club 1879
2   Fairlynch Museum history

Chapter 11   Vestryman
1   East Budleigh church records
2   Devon Record OfficeManuscript volume containing notes on church, memorial inscriptions and extracts from churchwardens' accounts, 1656-1694, by John Ingle Dredge and T N Brushfield, c1890 4344A/add99/PW/3
3   40 Commonplace books in the Devon Studies Library

Chapter 12   Antiquary
1   Sources: Eighteenth Century Exeter by Robert Newton, Andrew Brice and the Early Exeter Newspaper Press by T N Brushfield 1885, Antiquarian Notes and Queries, Devon and Cornwall Notes and Queries, West Country Poets website, The Life and bibliography of Andrew Brice by T N Brushfield MD and the Devon   Library   Local   Studies   website
2   Devon Record Office

2423A/add99/PW/1 Extracts from accounts, transcribed by T.N.

References

Brushfield, c.1890

3368A/add/PZ/57 Note about T.N. Brushfield, with small portrait
3788A/PZ/35

Transcript of churchwardens' accounts, 1537-1631 transcribed by H.T. Ellacombe and copied by T.H. Brushfield from a transcript.c. 1890

4344A/add99/PW/4

Transcript of churchwardens' accounts, 1555-1647, by T.N. Brushfield, c1890.

4344A/add99/PW/4 Transcript of churchwardens' accounts, 1555-1647, by T.N. Brushfield, c1890

4344A/add99/PW/5

Transcript of Churchwardens' accounts, 1648-1786, by T.N. Brushfield, c1890

Z19/15/5a-j

Commonplace books of T N Brushfield (10 volumes in box file)

Z19/17/3a-d Lectures and notes on obsolete punishments by T N Brushfield (4 vols)

Z19/36/14 Account book of household expenses of John Hayne of Exeter (1605-1643)

London Metropolitan records:Two letters from F C Hingeston Randolph to Dr Brushfield regarding the interpretation of the word "coast". Book bears bookplate of T N Brushfield on which has been written Exeter City Council 1911. MS is printed in TDA XXXIII (1901),pp187-269

References

3   Z19/7/8 Lectures on Sir Walter Ralegh by T N Brushfield

4   Sources: Eighteenth Century Exeter by Robert Newton, Andrew Brice and the Early Exeter Newspaper Press by T N Brushfield 1885, Antiquarian Notes and Queries, Devon and Cornwall Notes and Queries, West Country Poets website, The Life and bibliography of Andrew Brice by T N Brushfield MD and the Devon Library Local Studies website

The Mobiad - an heroi-com work - combining the heroic and the ludicrous; denoting high burlesque; as, a heroicomic poem.

5. The following are the principal authorities: Churches of Derbyshire (1875-9), by the Rev. Dr. Cox ; Christian .Symbolism, by J. Romilly Allen (1887); Gothic Ecclesiastical Architecture (1882), by M. Bloxam; Archteoloyia \ Parker's (Uossary ; and the various volumes of the Reliquary.

6. Transactions of the Devonshire Association, 1903.

Chapter 13 Raleghana

1   http://www.history-timelines.org.uk

2.   Biograph. Britan. (1760), VI, 3484-5.

J. Berkenhout, Biograph. Lit. (1777) â€" a list of 26 works.

A. Cayley, Life of Sir W. R. (1806), 11, 187-193. 1886.

3. Extracts from the Dictionary of National Biography, 1885-1900, Volume 47

Ralegh, Walter (1552?-1618) John Knox Laughton and Sidney Lee

Chapter 14 Memberships

(Devon and Cornwall Notes and Queries, 1910-11, vi. 161; private information; personal

References

knowledge)   H. T-S

Notes to Appendices
I   Proceedings of the Huguenot Society
Taken from 'The Commercial Life of a Suffolk Town, Framlingham around 1900'
by John Bridges
John Ogilby and William Morgan, Survey of the City of London, 1676
John Rocque, Plan of the cities of London and Westminster and Borough of Southwark, 1746
Richard Horwood, Map of London, Westminster and Southwark Shewing Every House, 1799
Census reports 1871
Pall Mall Gazette, 10th September 1888
The Jack the Ripper A-Z; Paul Begg, Martin Fido, Keith Skinner (Headline 1996)
given in Ralph L. Finn's 1963 memoir of a Jewish oyhood in the East End:
IV   John Rocque, Plan of the cities of London and Westminster and Borough of Southwark, 1746
Richard Horwood, Map of London, Westminster and Southwark Shewing Every House, 1799
Census reports 1871
Pall Mall Gazette, 10th September 1888
The Jack the Ripper A-Z; Paul Begg, Martin Fido, Keith Skinner (Headline 1996)

given in Ralph L. Finn's 1963 memoir of a Jewish boyhood in the

References

East End:

Trade directories of Londeon Birmingham and the Midlands and entries in the censu for 1841, 1951 and 1961. daughter of References John Ogilby and William Morgan, Survey of the City of London

Registry Report for Thomas Nadauld Brushfield

1. Thomas Nadauld BRUSHFIELD was born on 10/Dec/1828.
He died on 28/Nov/
1910 in Budleigh Salterton, Devonshire.
Hannah DAVIS daughter of John Davis[2] was born in 1834 in
Spitalfields, Middlesex.
She died in 1917 in Budleigh Salterton, Devon, England.
Notes for Hannah DAVIS:
Lived at The Cliff until TN died in 1910 then moved to Marine
Drive until she died in 1917
aged 83
Thomas Nadauld BRUSHFIELD and Hannah DAVIS were
married on 05/Aug/1857 in
Spitalfields, Middlesex.They had the following children:

    i. Archibald N Brushfield was born about 1870 in Woking,
Surrey, England
married Eveline D N NUGENT about Sep/1915 in Halifax,
Yorkshire. He
died about 1960 in Chichester, Sussex, England.
    ii. Percy Richard Valentine Brushfield was born in Mar/1861 in
Great
Boughton, Cheshire, United Kingdom. He died in 1873 in
Guildford.
    iii. Sydney Francis Brushfield was born about 1866. He died in
Jan/1889 in St Thomas, Devonshire, United Kingdom (Age at
Death: 23)
    iv. Eleanor Miller Brushfield was born in 1874 in Whitechapel,
Middlesex. She married Ernest George COWARD about

Dec/1901 in

St Thomas, Devon. She died in Jun/1957 in New Forest,
Hampshire,

England (Age at Death: 82).

v. Helena Brushfield was born about 1876 in Brookwood,
Surrey,

England.

vi.Dr Thomas N Brushfield was born in 1858 in Spitalfields,
Middlesex, England.

He married Susanna Russell on 25/Sep/1894. He died on
17/May/

1937 in Hastings, Sussex, England[28].

Notes for Thomas N Brushfield:

Discovered "Brushfield spots". Educated Cambridge Trinity
College

Adm. at CAIUS, Jan. 1877. S. and h. of Thomas Nadauld,
M.D., of

Brookwood Mount, Woking. B. 1858, at Upton-by-Chester.
School,

Guildford Grammar. Matric. Lent, 1877; B.A. 1880; M.A. and
M.B.

1888; M.D. 1924. At St George's Hospital, London. M.R.C.S.,
1886.

Medical Officer, Trinity House. Medical Officer of Health and
Surgeon

to the Admiralty, Scilly. In practice at Wimbledon, Surrey,
1898. At

Fountain Mental Hospital, Tooting Grove, S.W., in 1922. Died
May 17,

1937, aged 79, at 3, Highbury Mansions, St Leonards-on-Sea.
Brother

of the above. (Venn, II. 425; Medical Directory; The Times,
May 19,

1937.

vii. Florence Elizabeth Brushfield was born on 01/Nov/1862. She died in
1881.

viii. Edith Sarah Brushfield was born on 17/Jul/1867[29]. She died in
Mar/1948 in Surrey North Eastern, Surrey, England (Age at Death: 80)
Notes for Edith Sarah Brushfield:
General Notes:
Known as Buzzy

ix. Rosina Mary BRUSHFIELD (Mrs Shepherd) was born in 1859. She married Timothy
Shepard in 1899. She died in 1902.

x. Archibald N Brushfield was born about 1870 in Woking, Surrey, England He died
about 1960 in Chichester, Sussex, England.
Notes for Archibald N Brushfield:
General Notes:
Qualified as Doctor Married Eveline D N NUGENT who was born on 20/Dec/1890. She died in Dec/1975 in Chichester, West Sussex, England (Age at Death: 85)[30].
Archibald N Brushfield and Eveline D N NUGENT were married about Sep/1915 in
Halifax, Yorkshire.They had the following children:
i. Eleanor Brushfield was born about 1917.

ii. Thomas Nadauld Nugent BRUSHFIELD was born about Sep/1916 in
Halifax, Yorkshire. He died about Jun/1993 in Lancaster.

Sources:

1 Ancestry Family Trees (Online publication - Provo, UT, USA: Ancestry.com.

Registry report

Original

data: Family Tree files submitted by Ancestry members.), Ancestry.co.uk, http://
www.Ancestry.co.uk, Ancestry Family Tree.

2 Ancestry Family Trees (Online publication - Provo, UT, USA: Ancestry.com.
Original

data: Family Tree files submitted by Ancestry members.), Ancestry.co.uk, http://
www.Ancestry.co.uk, Ancestry Family Tree.

3 Ancestry Family Trees (Online publication - Provo, UT, USA: Ancestry.com.
Original

data: Family Tree files submitted by Ancestry members.), Ancestry.co.uk, http://
www.Ancestry.co.uk, Ancestry Family Tree.

4 1871 England Census (Ancestry.com. 1871 England Census [database on-line].
Provo,

UT, USA: Ancestry.com Operations Inc, 2004.), Class: RG10; Piece: 808; Folio: 9;
Page: 10; GSU roll: 838695.

5 England&Wales, Birth Index, 1916-2005 (Ancestry.com. England&Wales, Birth
Index,

1916-2005 [database on-line]. Provo, UT, USA: Ancestry.com Operations Inc, 2008.).

6 Ancestry Family Trees (Online publication - Provo, UT, USA: Ancestry.com.
Original

data: Family Tree files submitted by Ancestry members.), Ancestry.co.uk, http://
www.Ancestry.co.uk, Ancestry Family Tree.

7 1871 England Census (Ancestry.com. 1871 England Census [database on-line].
Provo,

UT, USA: Ancestry.com Operations Inc, 2004.), Class: RG10; Piece: 808; Folio: 9;
Page: 10; GSU roll: 838695.

8 England&Wales, Birth Index, 1916-2005 (Ancestry.com. England&Wales, Birth
Index,

1916-2005 [database on-line]. Provo, UT, USA: Ancestry.com Operations Inc, 2008.).

9 1871 England Census (Ancestry.com. 1871 England Census [database on-line].
Provo,

UT, USA: Ancestry.com Operations Inc, 2004.), Class: RG10; Piece: 808; Folio: 9;
Page: 10; GSU roll: 838695.

10 Ancestry Family Trees (Online publication - Provo, UT, USA: Ancestry.com.
Original

data: Family Tree files submitted by Ancestry members.), Ancestry.co.uk, http://
www.Ancestry.co.uk, Ancestry Family Tree.

11 England&Wales, Birth Index, 1916-2005 (Ancestry.com. England&Wales, Birth
Index,

Registry report

1916-2005 [database on-line]. Provo, UT, USA: Ancestry.com Operations Inc, 2008.).

12 Ancestry Family Trees (Online publication - Provo, UT, USA: Ancestry.com.
Original
data: Family Tree files submitted by Ancestry members.), Ancestry.co.uk, http://
www.Ancestry.co.uk, Ancestry Family Tree.

13

1871 England Census (Ancestry.com. 1871 England Census [database on-line]. Provo,
UT, USA: Ancestry.com Operations Inc, 2004.), Class: RG10; Piece: 808; Folio: 9;
Page: 10; GSU roll: 838695.

14 England&Wales, Birth Index, 1916-2005 (Ancestry.com. England&Wales, Birth
Index,
1916-2005 [database on-line]. Provo, UT, USA: Ancestry.com Operations Inc, 2008.).

15 England&Wales, FreeBMD Birth Index, 1837-1915 (FreeBMD. England&Wales,
FreeBMD Birth Index, 1837-1915 [database on-line]. Provo, UT, USA: Ancestry.com
Operations Inc, 2006.).

16 England&Wales, FreeBMD Death Index, 1837-1915 (FreeBMD. England&Wales,
FreeBMD Death Index, 1837-1915 [database on-line]. Provo, UT, USA: Ancestry.com
Operations Inc, 2006.).

17 England&Wales, Death Index, 1916-2006 (Ancestry.com. England&Wales, Death
Index,
1916-2006 [database on-line]. Provo, UT, USA: Ancestry.com Operations Inc, 2007.).

18 Ancestry Family Trees (Online publication - Provo, UT, USA: Ancestry.com.
Original
data: Family Tree files submitted by Ancestry members.), Ancestry.co.uk, http://
www.Ancestry.co.uk, Ancestry Family Tree.

19 1901 England Census (Ancestry.com. 1901 England Census [database on-line].
Provo,
UT, USA: Ancestry.com Operations Inc, 2005.), Class: RG13; Piece: 2026; Folio: 18;
Page: 28. Name: Helena Burchfield
Birth: abt 1875 in Brookwood, Surrey, England

20 1871 England Census (Ancestry.com. 1871 England Census [database on-line].
Provo,
UT, USA: Ancestry.com Operations Inc, 2004.), Class: RG10; Piece: 808; Folio: 9;

21 1891 England Census (Ancestry.com. 1891 England Census [database on-line].
Provo,

Registry report

UT, USA: Ancestry.com Operations Inc, 2005.), Class: RG12; Piece: 1274; Folio: 24; Page: 6; GSU roll: 6096384.

22 1871 England Census (Ancestry.com. 1871 England Census [database on-line]. Provo, UT, USA: Ancestry.com Operations Inc, 2004.), Class: RG10; Piece: 808; Folio: 9; Page: 10; GSU roll: 838695.

23 1891 England Census (Ancestry.com. 1891 England Census [database on-line]. Provo, UT, USA: Ancestry.com Operations Inc, 2005.), Class: RG12; Piece: 1274; Folio: 24; Page: 6; GSU roll: 6096384.

24 1891 England Census (Ancestry.com. 1891 England Census [database on-line]. Provo, UT, USA: Ancestry.com Operations Inc, 2005.), Class: RG12; Piece: 1274; Folio: 24; Page: 6; GSU roll: 6096384.

25 1871 England Census (Ancestry.com. 1871 England Census [database on-line]. Provo, UT, USA: Ancestry.com Operations Inc, 2004.), Class: RG10; Piece: 808; Folio: 9; Page: 10; GSU roll: 838695.

26 1871 England Census (Ancestry.com. 1871 England Census [database on-line]. Provo, UT, USA: Ancestry.com Operations Inc, 2004.), Class: RG10; Piece: 808; Folio: 9; Page: 10; GSU roll: 838695.

27 1891 England Census (Ancestry.com. 1891 England Census [database on-line]. Provo, UT, USA: Ancestry.com Operations Inc, 2005.), Class: RG12; Piece: 1274; Folio: 24; Page: 6; GSU roll: 6096384.

28 Cambridge University Alumni, 1261-1900 (Ancestry.com. Cambridge University Alumni, 1261-1900 [database on-line]. Provo, UT, USA: Ancestry.com Operations Inc, 1999.).

29 England&Wales, Death Index, 1916-2006 (Ancestry.com. England&Wales, Death Index, 1916-2006 [database on-line]. Provo, UT, USA: Ancestry.com Operations Inc, 2007.).

30 England&Wales, Death Index, 1916-2006 (Ancestry.com. England&Wales, Death Index, 1916-2006 [database on-line]. Provo, UT, USA: Ancestry.com Operations Inc, 2007.).

Registry report

31 Ancestry Family Trees (Online publication - Provo, UT, USA: Ancestry.com.
Original
data: Family Tree files submitted by Ancestry members.), Ancestry.co.uk, http://
www.Ancestry.co.uk, Ancestry Family Tree.

32 Ancestry Family Trees (Online publication - Provo, UT, USA: Ancestry.com.
Original
data: Family Tree files submitted by Ancestry members.), Ancestry.co.uk, http://
www.Ancestry.co.uk, Ancestry Family Tree.

Appendix I Huguenots in Britain

Who were the Huguenots? The origin of the word is obscure, but it was the name given in the 16th century to the Protestants in France, particularly by their enemies.

The impact of the Protestant Reformation was felt throughout Europe in the early 16th Century. Its greatest protagonists were the German Martin Luther and the Frenchman Jean Calvin. In France Calvinism penetrated all ranks of society, especially those of the literate craftsmen in the towns and of the nobility. There were eight civil wars in France between 1562 and 1598 - the Wars of Religion.

The charter of Edward VI (1547-53) enabled the first French protestant church to be set up in England. Descended from this church is the one in Soho square.

In 1589 the Protestant Henri de Bourbon, King of Navarre, inherited the French throne after the deaths of his three Valois cousins, sons of Catherine De Medici. Civil war continued, so in 1593, in the spirit of 'Paris is worth a Mass', Henri converted to Catholicism. Five years later the civil wars ended and Henri issued the Edict of Nantes which gave the Huguenots, his former co-religionists and comrades in arms, considerable privileges, including widespread religious liberty. Over time Huguenots became loyal subjects of the French crown.

However, their position became increasingly insecure as King Louis XIV, grandson of Henri IV, listened more and more to those who advised him that the existence of this sizeable religious minority was a threat to the absolute authority of the monarch. Gradually the Huguenots' privileges were eroded. In the 1680s Protestants in certain parts of France were deliberately terrorised by the billeting of unruly troops in their homes ['the Dragonnades']. Finally, in 1685

Louis revoked the Edict of Nantes, while exiling all Protestant pastors and at the same time forbidding the laity to leave France. To the considerable surprise of the government many did leave, often at great risk to themselves. Men who were caught, if not executed, were sent as galley slaves to the French fleet in the Mediterranean. Women were imprisoned and their children sent to convents.

About 200,000 Huguenots left France, settling in non-Catholic Europe - the Netherlands, Germany, especially Prussia, Switzerland, Scandinavia, and even as far as Russia where Huguenot craftsmen could find customers at the court of the Czars. The Dutch East India Company sent a few hundred to the Cape to develop the vineyards in southern Africa. About 50,000 came to England, perhaps about 10,000 moving on to Ireland. So there are many inhabitants of these islands who have Huguenot blood in their veins, whether or not they still bear one of the hundreds of French names of those who took refuge here - thus bringing the word 'refugee' into the English language.

Because of the political climate of the time, in a Britain strongly suspicious of the aims of Louis XIV's France, and in fact about to begin a series of wars to curb those ambitions, the Huguenots were on the whole welcomed here.

However, as the pamphlet literature of the time shows, they could not entirely escape the accusations levelled at immigrants from time immemorial -that their presence threatened jobs, standards of housing, public order, morality and hygiene and even that they ate strange foods! For at least half a century the Huguenots remained a recognisable minority, making their presence felt in banking, commerce, industry, the book trade, the arts and the army, on the stage and in teaching. Although many retained their Calvinist organisation and worship - treated more generously by government than home-grown nonconformity - by about 1760 they had ceased to stand out as foreign, even following the path of Anglican conformity in religion which some had taken from the very beginning.

source: Heugenot Society website

Appendix II Bibliography

The works of Dr Thomas Nadauld Brushfield:

1879 Certificates of Insanity

1890 Some Practical Hints on Symptoms, Treatments, and Medico-Legal Aspects of Insanity.

1888 A Bibliography of the Rev. George Oliver, D.D., of Exeter

1888 The Bishopric of Exeter, 1419 - 20: a Contribution to the History of the See

1888 Andrew Brice and the Early Exeter Newspaper Press

1888 Who Wrote the "Exmoor Scolding Stool?"

1893 Richard Izaclee and his "Antiquities of Exeter"
Devonshire Briefs, Parts I and II (1896)

1890 Description of a Perforated Stone Implement Found in the Parish of East Budleigh

1901 The Financial Diary of a Citizen of Exeter, 1631 - 43

1900 The British Archaeological Association new series VOL. VI.

1900 On Norman Tympana, with especial reference to those of Derbyshire

1899 Derbyshire Funeral Garlands
(Read at the Buxton Congress, July 19th, 1899.)

1899 Arbor Low
(Read at the Buxton Congress, July 20t/i, 1899.)

1900 Ashford Church

Thomas Brushfield also contributed further papers to the Devonshire Association:

1903 Britain's Burse or the New Exchange

1888 Notes on the Punishment known as the "Drunkard's Cloak" of Newcastle -on-Tyne

1888 Bygone Punishments

Papers that Dr Brushfield contributed to the Chester Archaeology Society's Journal which dealt with the same interest were:

1858 On Obsolete Punishments, with Particular Reference to those of Cheshire : Part I, The Brank, or Scold's Bridle

1886 Part II, The Ducking Stool and Allied punishments

1893 The Rows of Chester

1886 The Salmon Clause in the Indentures of Apprentices

Brushfield's other archaeological works are:

1905 Tideswell or Tidelow (Derbyshire Archaeological Society)

1889 Photograph of letter of Sir Walter Ralegh (Pros.,Soc. Antiquaries 1889)

1886 The Origen of the Surname of Brushfield ("The Reliquary")

1897 Yew Trees in Churchyards "Antiquities and Curiosities of the Church" ed. by W Andrews, 1897)

As one of the principal readers for Dr Murray's New English Dictionary he contributed 72,000 references for that work, of which 50,000 were accepted, making him the third largest contributor.

Appendix III London's East End
in the times of the Brushfields

David Perdue describes the conditions:

Until the second half of the 19th century London residents
were still drinking water from the very same portions of the
Thames that the open sewers were discharging into. Several
outbreaks of Cholera in the mid 19th century, along with The
Great Stink of 1858, when the stench of the Thames caused
Parliament to recess, brought a cry for action. Until 1854 it
was widely thought that disease was spread through foul air or
miasma. It seemed obvious to the Victorians, even the learned
ones, that if it stinks, it must be causing disease.

When cholera broke out in the Soho area in 1854 Dr. John Snow
teamed with Rev. Henry Whitehead to prove that the disease was
spread, not through foul odors and bad air, but by contaminated
water. Cholera is spread simply by one human digesting the
bacteria in the excrement of other infected humans. Snow and
Whitehead solved this riddle, not by direct study of the bacteria,
but by spatially projecting pedestrian patterns of where residents
got their drinking water. By this method they were able to show
that all of the cholera victims in the area drank from the same
Broad Street pump. The well had been contaminated with raw
sewage coming from the homes of cholera sufferers. The pump
handle was removed, and the epidemic ended. The story is in

Steven Johnson's *The Ghost Map*.

The recently established Metropolitan Police was a necessary reaction to the lawlessness of the East End of London and the streets around Spitalfields were known as very much part of the most difficult areas. The social scene was changing though and these were exciting times: in 1832 The Great Reform Act changed Parliamentary constituencies and the Factory Act revolutionised working conditions. During this time the Tolpuddle Martyrs were sentenced and Britain abolished slavery. The sweat shops around the market were little changed though and the poverty of the miserable dark and damp rooms filled with immigrant workers' families were much in evidence.

David perdue writes about this:

> At night the major streets are lit with feeble gas lamps. Side and secondary streets may not be lit at all and link bearers are hired to guide the traveler to his destination. Inside, a candle or oil lamp struggles against the darkness and blacken the ceilings.

London's East End was a poor place as Henry Mayhew described in his ***London Labour and London Poor*** :

> Pigs and cows in back yards, noxious trades like boiling tripe, melting tallow, or preparing cat's meat, and slaughter houses, dustheaps, and 'lakes of putrefying night soil' added to the filth.

London's East End has always had a dark side. On the surface, we think of it as a tight-knit community inhabited by chirpy Cockney barrow boys and flower girls, playfully peppering their sales patter with rhyming slang. But beneath that is a more sinister tale: one of overcrowding, poverty, violent crime, grimy industry and social unrest. This is the East End that emerged in the Victorian Age and that lingers still in the popular imagination.

East London has always been the poor relation of the West End. From the earliest times, it attracted trade and industry, thanks to its proximity to both The Thames and the River Lea. In particular, 'dirty' industries like tanning and tallow works clustered in the east, downwind and outside the city walls where 'noxious' trades were banned.

Despite this, the area remained a relatively pleasant place to live and work. That is, until the Victorian age…

As the British Empire expanded under Queen Victoria, so did trade and heavy industry. In 1827, the new St Katherine Docks opened, and with it, the need for large numbers of dock workers. There was no shortage in the East End. Alongside a swelling local population, the area had long attracted immigrants fleeing political unrest and religious persecution: most notably, Jews and French Huguenots in the 17th century. Between 1870 and 1914 they were joined by thousands of Jewish settlers from Poland, Romania and Russia who fled to England to escape Tsarist pogroms.

The elegant Huguenot houses of Spitalfields were divided up into tiny, inadequate dwellings, and even newly-built housing soon became over-crowded and run down. Wages were pitiful, thanks to unscrupulous employment practices such as casual labour and piecework. Disease was rife: in 1866, a cholera epidemic swept the

East End, killing 3,000 people.

Those who could claw their way above the poverty line soon moved out – aided by the arrival of the railways – leaving behind the highest concentration of the poor and underprivileged anywhere in London. When social reformer Charles Booth produced his extensive survey of the living conditions of the poor in 1887, he concluded that 13% of the East End population was chronically poor and, of those, "a part must be considered separately, as the class for whom decent life is not imaginable."

No wonder then, that crime, immorality, drunkenness and violence were so rife. Gangs, prostitutes and robbers roamed the unlit alleys that, by the late 19th century, had become known as 'The Abyss'.

Perhaps the area's darkest moment came in the late summer and early autumn of 1888, when Jack the Ripper carried out a series of grisly murders on Whitechapel prostitutes. He was never caught.

AETN UK

Spitalfields takes its name from the hospital and priory, St. Mary's Spittel that was founded in 1197. Lying in the heart of the East End, it is an area known for its spirit and strong sense of community. It was in a field next to the priory where the now famous market first started in the thirteenth century.

As an international city, London is celebrated for its diversity in population. The East End has always been recognised for the wealth of cultures represented. Spitalfields served as a microcosm of this polyglot society, the 'melting pot' fusion of east and west. Historically, it has played host to a transient community – primarily for new immigrants.

Spitalfields had been relatively rural until the Great Fire of London.

By 1666, traders had begun operating beyond the city gates – on the site where today's market stands. The landmark Truman's Brewery opened in 1669 and in 1682 King Charles II granted John Balch a Royal Charter giving him the right to hold a market on Thursdays and Saturdays in or near Spital Square.

The success of the market encouraged people to settle in the area and following the edict of Nantes in 1685, Huguenots fleeing France brought their silk weaving skills to Spitalfields. Their grand houses can still be seen around what is now the conservation area of Fournier Street. Today these houses are home to many artists including Gilbert and George and Trcy Emin.

The Huguenots were soon followed by Irish labourers in the mid-1700s escaping the potato famine, many of whom would work on the construction of the nearby London docks. As the area grew in popularity, Spitalfields became a parish in its own right in 1729 when Hawkesmoor's Christ Church was consecrated.

The Irish were followed by East European Jews escaping the Polish pogroms and harsh conditions in Russia; as well as entrepreneurial Jews from the Netherlands. From the 1880s to 1970s Spitalfields was overwhelmingly Jewish and probably one of the largest Jewish communities in Europe with over 40 Synagogues.

By the middle of the 20th century the Jewish community had mostly moved on. Since 1970s a thriving Bangladeshi community has flourished in the area. Bringing new cultures, trades and business to the area including the famous Brick Lane restaurant district.

Evidence of the people and communities that have given the area it's unique character can still be seen - a Huguenot church, a Methodist chapel, a Jewish synagogue, and Muslim mosque stand among traditional and new shops, restaurants, markets and homes.

source; www.spitalfields.co.uk website

Appendix IV Scandalous Treatment
of the Insane

Due, perhaps, to the absence of a centralized state response to the social problem of madness until the nineteenth-century, private madhouses proliferated in eighteenth-century England on a scale unseen elsewhere. References to such institutions are limited for the seventeenth-century but it is evident that by the start of the eighteenth-century the so-called 'trade in lunacy' was well established.

Daniel Defoe, an ardent critic of private madhouses, estimated in 1724 that there were fifteen then operating in the London area. Defoe may have exaggerated but exact figures for private metropolitan madhouses are only available from 1774 when licensing legislation was introduced and sixteen institutions were recorded.

As Defoe said of the morals of the time:

Whenever God erects a house of prayer,
The devil always builds a chapel there;
And 'twill be found, upon examination,
The latter has the largest congregation.
The True-Born Englishman: A Satire (1701)

At least two of these, Hoxton House and Wood's Close, Clerkenwell, had been in operation since the seventeenth-century. By 1807, the number had only increased to seventeen. It is conjectured that this limited growth in the number of London madhouses is likely to reflect the fact that vested interests, especially the College of Physicians, exercised considerable control in preventing new entrants to the market. Thus, rather than a proliferation of private madhouses in London, existing institutions tended to expand considerably in size. The establishments which increased most during the eighteenth-century, such as Hoxton House, did so by accepting pauper patients rather than private, middle-class, fee-paying patients. Significantly, pauper patients, unlike their private counterparts, were not subject to inspection under the 1774 legislation.

Fragmentary evidence indicates that some provincial madhouses were in existence in England from at least the seventeenth-century and possibly earlier.

A madhouse at Box, Wiltshire had opened during the seventeenth-century and further early businesses include one at Guildford in Surrey which was accepting patients by 1700, one at Fonthill Gifford in Wiltshire from 1718, another at Hook Norton in Oxfordshire from about 1725, one at St Albans dating from around 1740 and a madhouse at Fishponds in Bristol from 1766. It is likely that many of these provincial madhouses, as was the case with the exclusive Ticehurst House, may have evolved from householders who were boarding lunatics on behalf of parochial authorities and later formalised this practice into a business venture.

The vast majority were small in scale with only seven asylums outside of London with in excess of thirty patients by 1800 and somewhere between and ten and twenty institutions had fewer patients than this.

Throughout the 18th and early 19th century, physicians still believed in the Ancient Greek principle that the body was governed by four 'humours': blood, phlegm, yellow bile and black bile. Too much black bile in the body was said to cause madness in the form of melancholy or mania.

Treatment for the 'insane' during this period was dominated by the attempt to rectify the humoral imbalances through evacuative remedies: bleeding, blisters, purging (emptying the bowel) and vomiting. Although this therapy appears barbaric today, it followed approved medical practices of the time.

Bethlem, was however, condemned in its application of treatment ('physick'), which was seen as both arbitrary and violent. It was not until 1772 that the attendance of medical officers was required in the administration of purges and vomits. Bethlem's management, in giving unqualified and over-stretched staff this control, was in dire need of reform.

The scandalous discovery in 1814 of the Bethlem patient James Norris, who had been restrained in chains for fourteen years, was central to the Parliamentary inquiry into 'madhouses' of 1815/16.

Mechanical restraints and strait-jackets were widely used at Bethlem, but were generally seen as a necessity rather than a cure. With roughly 260 patients in the 1760s, the skeleton staff of ten or eleven used restraint to prevent 'the most violent' patients 'from doing mischief to themselves' or others.

The routine dosing of patients, for sedative reasons, was also in common use at Bethlem. The Bethlem physician Richard Hale

(1670-1728) was even praised for handling maniacs not so much 'with chains and bars, as by sedating them'. Dosing, however, did little more than mask the symptoms.

Despite some aspects of genuine innovation in patient care during the reign of the Monro dynasty, their entrenchment in Bethlem for over 120 years, led to conservative treatment. Practices were, in general, unquestioningly handed down from father to son, with little attempt to pioneer new therapies.

The Moorfields building, the second home of Bethlem Hospital from 1676 until 1815, was one of the grandest in the city and lavishly ornamented. Design and function were influenced by Bethlem's growing popularity as a London show.

Patients were forbidden to use the front garden, as this would have necessitated a rise in wall height, so obscuring the view for the passer-by. By 1770, this public sight-seeing was deemed inhumane and finally stopped.

Bethlem initially housed 120 patients. The majority had individual cells – '12 feet by 8 feet 10 inches', which lacked glazing, while the patients had only inadequate clothing. Cold was traditionally viewed as having a sedative effect upon the patients, and eliminated the dangers of over-heating the brain.

The Parliamentary inquiry into madhouses of 1815/16, criticised the cold and damp conditions of Bethlem. Even when the hospital moved to its new home at St. George's Field, Southwark, the windows were still unglazed. The Governors believing this dissipated 'the disagreeable effluvias peculiar to all madhouses'. Glass was finally fitted in 1816.

Rudimentary water supplies and the lack of latrines in both buildings led to dirty and unhygienic conditions, yet staff attempted to maintain a sanitary environment. That the Parliamentary enquiry found 'the apartments in general...to be clean, and the patients who were not confined tolerably comfortable', reflects that Bethlem was, in cleanliness, no different to other institutions at the time.

It was the discovery of the side rooms that was the shocking revelation within the inquiry. Here, incontinent or 'highly irritated' patients prone to tearing their clothes, lay virtually naked, chained to their straw beds.

As early as 1684 a matron was employed at Bethlem so that 'the poore Lunatikes there be kept sweet and clean'. However, even after the move to new premises in 1816, there was much room for improvement at Bethlem.

During the 1815/16 Parliamentary enquiry into 'madhouses', the medical officers at Bethlem Royal Hospital were cross-examined on their use of mechanical restraints. The 1815 Select Committee agreeing ultimately, that restraints were used 'much beyond what is necessary'.

John Haslam, Bethlem's apothecary, opposed the use of strait-jackets stating that:

> The hands are completely secured if the strait-waistcoat be tied tightly, respiration is prevented or impeded, and it is always at the mercy of the keeper how tight he chooses to tie the waistcoat. If the patient be irritated by itching in any part, he is unable to administer the relief by scratching, or if

troubled by flies in hot weather, it is a painful encumbrance, and if not changed is liable to absorb a great deal of perspiration, which renders sometimes the skin excoriated.

Thomas Monro, Bethlem's physician, and most other witnesses at the 1815 enquiry, considered strait-jackets to be better than chains. Monro, however, also distanced himself from this practice:

I have nothing in the world to do with the irons; I never gave orders for the patients to be put into irons in the whole course of my life...[chains and fetters] are fit only for pauper lunatics: if a gentleman was put in irons, he would not like it.

Monro's testimony worryingly suggests that the use of chains was determined by class rather than medical grounds.

Situated variously in Bishopsgate, Moorfields and Lambeth, one of the main attractions over the centuries for the London mob was the Bethlehem Royal Hospital or Bedlam'.

So famous has the hospital become that the word has been accepted into the English language signifying 'a scene of wild uproar'.

The lunatic asylum made a lot of money from the public up to the year 1770, as visitors were admitted to see the lunatics as we might visit the zoo today, the entrance fee being 1d.

In a report to the House of Commons in 1815, Dr. Connoly reported that he found in one of the side-rooms; "about ten patients each chained by one arm or leg to the wall, each wearing a sort of dressing gown with nothing to fasten it.

Some were sensible and accomplished, some were imbeciles. Many women were locked up naked with only one blanket."

One inmate was chained to her bed for eight years, the matron feeling the prisoner would murder her if released.

When finally the date of her release arrived she became tranquil, nursing two dolls which she imagined were her children. Another patient, well-known to the many visitors, wore a straw cap and promised to declare war on the stars if rewarded with a bottle of wine.

One of the most famous patients, often visited by members of Parliament was a certain William Morris. For twelve years he was chained with a strong iron ring round his neck His arms were pinioned by an iron bar and he could only move twelve feet away from the wall. In this position he lived as normal a life as possible before dying shortly after his release.

Two more patients spent a total of over eighty years between them in Bedlam for trying to kill the same man. James Hadfield was confined for 39 years for attempting to shoot George III.

He spent his time writing verses on the deaths of his cats and birds, his only companions in the hospital. Margaret Nicholson spent 42 years in solitary confinement for attempting to stab the same King.

William Cooper described his thoughts on visiting the asylum as a youngster:

"The madness of some of them has such a humorous air, and displayed itself in so many whimsical freaks, that it was impossible not to be entertained at the same time that I was angry with myself for being so."

The life stories of some of the patients who finished their days in Bedlam make fascinating reading.

Hannah Hyson died within days of being rescued by her father from Bethlem, her body covered in scabs and her knuckles red raw where she had crawled about her cell on her hands and knees.

Ann Morley, a former patient at Bethlem, was admitted to Northampton Asylum in a skeletally weak condition, incontinent, prolapsed and close to death.

Upon recovery, she testified to being punched in the face by a bad-tempered nurse called Black Sall (the name referred to Sall's moods), hosed down with freezing water and being made to sleep naked on straw in a cellar.

It was only with the arrival of William Charles Hood, in 1853, that Bethlem began its long process of reform, and even after this date episodes of cruelty and neglect surfaced, with a high suicide rate attracting press coverage in the 1880s.

Victorian society emphasized female purity and supported the ideal of the "true woman" as wife, mother, and keeper of the home. In Victorian society, the home was the basis of morality and a sanctuary free from the corruption of the city. As guardian of the home and family, women were believed to be more emotional, dependent, and gentle by nature. This perception of femininity led to the popular conclusion that women were more susceptible to disease and illness, and was a basis for the diagnosis of insanity in many female patients during the 19th century.

On the basis of Victorian gender distinctions, it was common for female patients to be diagnosed as suffering from hysteria. 19th century upper and middle class women were completely dependent on their husbands and fathers, and their lives revolved around their role as respectable daughter, housewife, and mother. With so little power, control, and independence, depression, anxiety, and stress were common among Victorian women struggling to cope with a static existence under the thumb of strict gender ideals and unyielding patriarchy.

Characterized by nervous, eccentric, and erratic behaviour, the epidemiology of hysteria eluded medical explanation in the Victorian era. Although there were hysterical males, attributing the condition to the female nature fit the social model of women, and validated the medical integrity of psychiatry by providing a suitable diagnosis. For hysterical women and their families, the asylum offered a convenient and socially acceptable excuse for inappropriate, and potentially scandalous behaviour. Rather than being viewed as a bad and immoral woman, honour and reputation could be maintained by the diagnosis of a medical condition and commitment to an asylum.

References: Bringing Back in Victorian England: Pauper Lunatics, 1840- 1870' in Bynum, Porter & Shepherd. (eds.)

1728 by Daniel Defoe. ... about unjust declarations of insanity, about strange views on mental illness

Appendix V   Works of Sir Walter Ralegh
(1552? - 1618)

Poetry

In Commendation of The Steel Glass
The Excuse
An Epitaph Upon The Right Honourable Sir Philip Sidney
A Vision Upon This Conceit of The Fairy Queen.
Another of the Same
The Nymph's Reply to the Shepherd
Farewell to the Court [Like truthless dreams]
Sir Walter Ralegh to his Son [The Wood, the Weed, the   Wag]
On the Cards and Dice
The Silent Lover
The Lie
To the Translator of Lucan
On the Life of Man [What is our life? a play of passion]
The Passionate Man's Pilgrimage
As You Came from the Holy Land
Even Such Is Time
Praised be Diana's Fair and Harmless Light
[Like to a hermit]
A description of love [Now what is love?]
[Nature, that washed her hands in milk]

The Ocean to Cynthia (before 1603)

Of Questionable Attribution

Epitaph on the Earl of Leicester
A Farewell to the Vanities of the World

Prose

The Last Fight of the Revenge (1591)
The Discovery of Guiana (1595)
A Discourse Touching a War with Spain (1603)
The History of the World (1614)
The Prerogative of Parliaments (1615)
Sir Walter Ralegh's Instructions to his Son
and to Posterity (pub. 1632)
A Discourse of the Original and Fundamental
Cause of Natural War (1615? pub. 1650)
A Discourse of the Invention of Ships, Anchors,
          Compass, &c. (1615? pub. 1650)

Observations Concerning the Royal Navy
and Sea-service (<1612; pub. 1650)
Sir Walter Ralegh's Apology for his
Voyage to Guiana (1617? pub. 1650)
The Sceptic (pub. 1651)
Causes of the Magnificency and Opulence

of Cities (pub. 1651)

On the Seat of Government (pub. 1651)

Observations Touching Trade & Commerce, &c.
(pub. 1653)

The Reign of King William the I,
entitled The Conqueror (1617? pub. 1693)

A Treatise of the Soul (pub. 1829)

The Interest of England with Regard to Foreign Alliances
explained in two discourses (1611? pub. 1750)

   1. Concerning a match between the Lady Elizabeth
     and the Prince of Piedmont

   2. Touching a marriage between Prince Henry of England
     and a daughter of Savoy

Works Spuriously Attributed to Ralegh

The Prince, or Maxims of State (pub. 1642)
The Cabinet-council (pub. 1658)

Other

Ralegh's Farewell Letter to his Wife Before Dying
Some Ralegh poems translated into Russian- E&Y Feldman
Some Ralegh poems translated into French - B. Hoepffner

Index

Index

Dr Foster 150
Dr J H Moreton 25
Dr Millar 25
Dr Murray 114
Dr Walker 84
Dr. Diamond 57
Dr. Llewelyn Jones 45
Dr. W. C. Minor 72
Drake 82
Drury Lane 116
Duke of Wellington 41
Duke Street 2
Earl of Desmond 131
Earl of Essex 137
Earl of Shaftesbury 126
East Budleigh 81
East Devon 82
Eastern Dispensary 41
Edge Stone Head 7
Edmund Gosse 146
Edmund Spenser 131
Edward Edwards 145
Edward Sackett 62
Elizabeth Brushfield 7
Esther Payne 77
Euston Station 32
Exeter Post-Boy 114
Exmouth 93
F. J. Furnivall 74
Fort Street) 2
Fournier Street 2
Fox Talbot 57
Francis W. Stevens 22

Acknowledgements

This book was written at home, in Devon, with the help of friends interested in the literary history of Budleigh Salterton. The members of the Fairlynch Museum Trust and its chairman provided access to its archive. The Devon Heritage Centre opened its extensive collection of Brushfield papers held in the studies libraries in Exeter and Barnstaple.

The Welcome Trust kindly allowed the use of the lithograph described as that of *a contemporary lunatic in a French Asylum* from their collection. Michael Wickenden kindly asssisted with the genealogy of the Brushfield family.

Mrs Jean Brushfield and other family members provided an insight into their extended history for use in the book.

Joy Gawne delved into her Budleigh archive of memorabilia to include advertisements for plays produced in the town by Dr Brushfield.

The libraries of Birmingham University and the Oxford University Press provided details of correspondence relating to the OED.

Other invaluable insights into Thomas Brushfield's days in Budleigh came from the papers of the Clinton Devon Estates.

Finally it is to Brenda, my lifelong partner, that I owe the most in this as in so much else.

Printed in Great Britain
by Amazon

30888378R00126